W9-CNW-765

MANDATE
FOR
CANADA

MANDATE
FOR
CANADA

JOHN CRISPO

General Publishing Co. Limited
Don Mills, Ontario

First published 1979 by
General Publishing Co. Limited
30 Lesmill Road
Don Mills, Ontario

First printing

Cover design by Robin Taviner

Canadian Cataloguing in Publication Data

Crispo, John H.G., 1933 -
 Mandate for Canada

ISBN 0-7736-1051-0

I. Canada - Social conditions. 2. Canada - Politics and government. 3. Canada - Economic conditions.
I. Title

HN103.5.C75   309.1'71   C79-094405-7

ISBN 0-7736-1051-0
Printed and bound in Canada

Contents

Preface

IT IS OBVIOUSLY presumptuous for any one individual to think that he could produce "a mandate for Canada." Yet I have tried to do so, while acknowledging that my particular mandate is neither complete nor definitive. It is certainly not the last word.

I have been driven to attempt this task by my profound concern about the future of this country. Throughout this volume I will be repeatedly stressing the difference between this country's actual and potential performance. We have so much going for us, and yet we have failed to take full advantage of it. I find it frustrating beyond words to live with this unnecessary shortcoming.

This volume is a personal political commentary. It represents years of thinking about the challenges that beset us. Only recently have I found it possible to pull all my ideas together. While I am conscious of many persons who have helped me over the years with these ideas, there are doubtless many more to whom I am subconsciously indebted.

But the final product is mine, as best indicated by the absence of any footnotes or quotations. I must take the blame for any foolhardiness, and the credit for any wisdom, that the reader may find on these pages.

John Crispo

CHAPTER ONE

The Canadian Challenge

THIS IS A time of serious, national soul-searching in Canada. While this soul-searching has been sparked by the threat of Québec's separation, the real causes go much deeper, reflecting the fact that this country is confronted by a series of crises.

These crises range over the entire socio-economic-political spectrum. They embrace not just the separatist threat in Québec, but also the challenges posed by our other provincial and regional disparities. They include the difficulties besetting our economic system as it suffers from the interrelated problems of sluggish growth, high unemployment, and persistent inflation. Not to be minimized either are risks to our social fabric as we strive to bring our social security and welfare spending under control.

As if all this were not enough, we have a host of other problems ranging from the need to find a more satisfactory balance between civil liberties and national security to the search for a new industrial strategy and/or trade policy for this country. In addition, we must also restrain the excessive influence which civil service bureaucracies and regulatory tribunals seem to wield over us.

These and other forces at work in our country help explain why so many of our major institutions are experiencing a credibility gap. Month by month, it is largely a question of which leading institution is the most suspect in the minds of the public. Cumulatively, it is almost as if our whole society and our very way of life were on the line.

There is no escape from these challenges by trying to ignore them. They are too pervasive. Rather, one must attempt to come to grips with them. This is the exciting part about our times. We have no choice now but to face up to our problems. This could provide us with the opportunity of a lifetime to be involved in the reordering of our priorities and the reshaping of our future. This is the spirit in which I have written this volume.

Some Underlying Assumptions

Aside from a belief in Canada as a continuing national entity, there are a series of values and institutions which I would argue are basic to our present way of life. Certainly, they are critical to my thinking as it is reflected throughout this work.

First and foremost are what one can best describe as fundamental Western values. These values have traditionally included freedom of assembly, press, religion, and speech; the right to own private property; and the sanctity of contracts. More recently, lip service, at least, has been paid to freedom from human degradation, poverty, and suffering, and to the ideal of equality of opportunity. In fact, these latter values remain so weak in the total scheme of things that they do not serve as an adequate complement for the earlier and more traditional values.

Liberal democracy is another vital component of the hierarchy of values and institutions which make up our present system. In essence, liberal democracy may be described as government of, by, and for the people. But much more is involved than this succinct phrase implies. For example, the executive and legislative branches of a liberal democratic government may take a congressional or parliamentary form, or some combination of the two. In any event, the existence of a bill of rights and an independent judiciary is an indispensable part of such a system. Otherwise, the power of government vis-à-vis other groups and individuals in society could prove intolerable.

The next level in this hierarchy of values and institutions is much more debatable. With history to bear me out, I would argue that there is no way of sustaining a liberal democratic system except by combining it with something like a competitive, enterprise, or market economic system. This type of system may also be termed mixed free enterprise or modified capitalism. However described, what I have in mind is a system in which the interaction of buyers and sellers of different goods and services in the marketplace is still more influential in determining what is consumed and produced than government decisions, fiats, or regulations.

Mixed free enterprise or modified capitalism can take a variety of forms. At one extreme, there is North American capitalism which may be described as "capitalism with a vengeance." This is the dog-eat-dog version of capitalism in which anything goes as long as one is not

caught doing it. At the other extreme is the model of
capitalism which existed ten to fifteen years ago in
Sweden and which could be characterized as "capitalism
with a conscience." This brand of capitalism functioned
within a social democratic framework which allowed
capitalism a relatively free hand while using the proceeds
to eradicate poverty and to narrow income differentials.
Unfortunately, the benefactors of this system in Sweden
could not restrain themselves and milked it to the point of
undermining the incentives and motivations which have
always made capitalism so productive.

Regardless of the form which mixed free enterprise or
modified capitalism takes, it is unlikely to survive unless
complemented by a reasonably free and unfettered
collective bargaining system. Workers will not accept
their employers charging what the traffic will bear in the
absence of having a similar opportunity to do so. Since
few workers have sufficient power to pursue this goal on
their own, many of them are bound to join with their
fellow workers in a common front for collective bargaining purposes.

To this end, workers require independent unions free
of management or government influence. Otherwise,
there can be no meaningful collective bargaining. This is
why a strong labor movement is also an integral part of
the total system I have been describing.

In championing this hierarchy of values and institutions, I do not mean to suggest that either the hierarchy
as a whole or its components represent the ultimate for
which we should be striving. Far from it. Difficulties and
shortcomings plague every part. Nevertheless, collectively if not individually, these values and institutions do
represent the least of many possible evils, which is no

mean accomplishment in this world of none-too-appealing alternatives.

Objective and Outline

The objective and purpose of this volume is, first of all, to clarify the problems and prospects confronting this country. After all, one cannot tackle any challenge effectively without an appreciation of its dimensions.

The very process of trying to identify the facts of life confronting this country helps to narrow the options that remain available to us. The longer one allows any problem to fester, the fewer the choices one usually has left. Since many of our problems have been with us for decades, the alternatives are not that plentiful.

Given the value judgments outlined above, the options from which I have to choose are even more limited. The difficulty I face is to seek answers or solutions which are not only reasonably consistent with these values, but also with each other. The ultimate objective of this volume is to offer just such a coherent package of proposals — impossible as that task may seem.

The first substantive chapter of this book, is entitled "The Canadian Paradox." It features the contrasting set of long-term opportunities and short-term problems which face this country. By its nature, it is a general chapter which does not begin to cover the full range of issues dealt with in the chapters that follow. Nonetheless, it does set the stage for most of them.

Each of the ensuing chapters deals with a particular issue or series of issues which I deem sufficiently important to warrant separate treatment. Except for the first of these chapters, no ranking is necessarily intended.

It need hardly be added that others would probably choose to deal with a different list and sequence of issues.

The first issue that I discuss revolves around the vital necessity of attracting a higher caliber of individual to serve in public office. This is a must if we are to begin to come to grips with our many other challenges. Yet, it won't be easy given the demanding and thankless nature of the politician's role. We can hope, though, that we can make the job attractive enough to encourage a more qualified range of candidates than we have in the past.

Then there is the contentious issue of a bill of rights. Should one be enshrined in our constitution? If so, what basic fundamental or traditional rights should be included? What about the controversial issue of language rights? In addition, there is the problem of reconciling civil liberties with domestic and national security, and the pressing matter of freedom of information in government.

In the federal-provincial sphere, the question is how decentralized we can afford to become. The pressure for decentralization in this country is not coming only from Québec, but from the new "have" or resource provinces. We must decide which federal powers are essential if Confederation is to remain viable, albeit in a more decentralized form.

Our parliamentary institutions are also suspect. What is required to make the present House of Commons a more meaningful and respected legislative assembly? What about the Senate? Is there any point in trying to reform it or should it just be abolished? Equally controversial questions revolve around the place of the monarchy, the use of referenda, and the role of the Supreme Court. Concern is also increasingly being expressed about the impact of the armies of civil servants, mandarins, and regulators who seem to intrude more and more into our daily lives.

On the economic side two issues currently dominate the scene. One is the purported need for some kind of an industrial strategy to replace our original national policy. The other relates to the continuing threat posed by inflation. The latter not only raises questions about the fiscal and monetary management of the country; it also raises the question of whether all manner of private interest groups or power blocs — be they in labor, management, the professions, or elsewhere — should be allowed to continue to run roughshod over the rest of us.

Beyond the political and economic arenas, there are many cultural and social issues to be tackled. Not the least of these pertains to the shape of Canadian nationalism whether in its English- or French-Canadian form or in some more common form. Regardless of its form or forms, the question is whether Canada can maintain any significant distinctiveness in the face of U.S. influence over this country.

In terms of social issues, there are basic issues to be decided concerning both our tax and social security systems. On the tax side, should we be moving away from ability to pay as the primary criterion in the raising of our government revenues? On the spending side, what about the concept of a guaranteed minimum income based on a negative income tax?

There are no easy or ready solutions to many of the problems I will be addressing. Despite the fact that many of my proposals are quite definitive and precise, I would be satisfied if they just pointed us in the right directions. In this sense, they might better be construed as general guidelines, rather than as specific recommendations.

CHAPTER TWO

The Canadian Paradox

THIS IS SUPPOSED to be Canada's century. It was for a time and still can be. This country continues to enjoy great advantages relative to most others in the world. The challenge is to begin realizing that potential once again. To do that we not only require an appreciation of our tremendous potential, but we also need a better understanding of what seems to have gone wrong. Such an appraisal can be approached from several different vantage points.

Canada: A Land of Almost Unlimited Potential

One of the considerations which prompted me to write this book is the bewilderment I discovered among Western Europeans about Canada's seeming inability to realize its potential. Western Europeans look with envy upon this land of plenty and cannot fathom how we can be managing it so badly.

What Western Europeans most envy about Canada are our resources and space. They are more impressed by the vastness of the country than they should be because they lack an appreciation of how limited the habitable area is. Yet even this area is great compared to our population. Thus, we start with an immense advantage because we have so much more land per capita.

When it comes to our resources, the view of Western Europeans reflects their own scarcity complex. Most of Western Europe has to import the bulk of its resources. Canada, in contrast, has the potential to be self-sufficient in its energy requirements and has bountiful raw materials with which to work. Our geography and topography have provided us with ample agricultural land as well as fisheries, forests, and most of the major minerals known to man.

Canada also has well-developed communications and transportation systems. These systems have helped weld the country together, despite its immense size. Much of the cost of these systems was incurred in the past, but they will continue to provide benefits for years to come.

Canada is also a remarkably civilized country. Its educated people live within a society which features highly developed judicial, political, and social systems. While these systems still leave much to be desired, they remain far ahead of those of most other countries in the world, if only in terms of a willingness to live and let live.

Finally, one of our greatest advantages is the fact that Canada shares the North American continent with a country which still represents the single most lucrative market in the world. Although close proximity with such a giant has its disadvantages, one should not minimize the advantages which have and could flow even more fully from access to the United States' market.

While other benefits enjoyed by this country can be

cited, enough should have been mentioned already to dispel the notion that we are anything but a favored nation. We are so well-endowed with almost everything which counts that it is truly amazing that we have not, at least in recent years, made better use of it.

On the other hand, one might well speculate on where we would be were we not citizens of such a rich land. It is almost as if no amount of mismanagement can put this country down. It has so many natural advantages that it cannot be run into the ground no matter how hard we try.

Canada: A Land of Shortfalls and Shortcomings

It is hard to know where to begin when assessing Canada's recent failure to live up to its potential. Perhaps the best place to start is with the lack of confidence and the uncertainty which have now plagued the country for several years. This lack of confidence and uncertainty have spread far beyond our borders to many foreigners who have come to wonder just where this country is heading.

However they got started, this lack of confidence and and this uncertainty may now be attributed to a host of disturbing developments. Among the most important of these are the following:

    i)   our constitutional crisis;
    ii)   our deep political malaise;
   iii)   continuing stagflation;
   iv)   our propensity to live beyond our means;
    v)   our related tendency to price ourselves out of world markets;
   vi)   the decline in the value of our dollar.

Our Constitutional Crisis. The division of powers between the federal and provincial governments has been a source of contention ever since these powers were spelled out in the BNA Act. Although the current variation on our perennial constitutional crisis has been brought to a head by the separatist threat in Québec, it has dimensions which extend far beyond that province's borders. As we shall see, the new "have" provinces are also determined to change the present distribution of power within Confederation.

As for Québec's separatists and their aspirations, they are not unlike those of similar movements all over the world. Wherever a significant minority group feels its language and culture are threatened, it is fighting to preserve them.

Originally, protection of the French-Canadian language and culture was left largely to the Catholic church. But this was at the price of undue clerical intervention which denied to most Québecois anything other than a classical education. This is one of the reasons why English Canadians and foreigners found it so easy to dominate the business and commercial life of Québec. These factors, in turn, helped set in motion the so-called Quiet Revolution — which is no longer so quiet.

Although René Lévesque and the Parti Québécois came to power largely because of public disenchantment with the apparent corruption and obvious incompetence of the previous Liberal regime, they quickly translated their mandate into a demand for separation. More recently, this has been softened to "sovereignty-association" — whatever that means. In all probability, it amounts to the same thing in the long run. Nonetheless, Lévesque and his confreres do seem content in the meantime to press for a realignment of federal-provincial powers.

This dovetails with similar pressures coming from the new Western "have" provinces, symbolized by Alberta. In their desire to secure more power in general and exclusive control over their resources in particular, they play into the hands of Québec separatists, albeit with a different purpose in mind. Only Ontario, which has always dominated Confederation, and some of the Maritime "have-not" provinces, which have become heavily dependent on equalization payments, have had much to say for the status quo.

Yet even our "have-not" provinces have many reasons for questioning the status quo. If Confederation was ever supposed to imply a social contract, they have every right to feel shortchanged. The economic disparities from which they suffer remain galling. Their countrymen in the wealthier provinces enjoy up to fifty percent higher incomes. And yet they pay lower municipal and provincial taxes and have better public and social services. Equalization payments only partially narrow these gaps. No wonder those in the "have-not" areas want a better deal.

Because of all the forces seeking changes in Canada's federal-provincial arrangements, there is great uncertainty about the future distribution of powers within this country. Since further decentralization of power seems unavoidable, there are growing doubts about the capacity of the federal government to play a central role in the management of our affairs. At the very least, this leads to searching questions about our ability to engage in effective federal-provincial and interprovincial co-operation.

In the absence of such cooperation, one has to wonder how we will manage to put in place a coherent set of policies in any area. The fact that we have already done so much to balkanize the country through a variety of interprovincial trade barriers is hardly encouraging.

Our Deep Political Malaise. Although the issue does not receive as much overt public attention as it might, Canada is also the victim of a deep political malaise. This is evident from the caliber of person who is willing to stand for public office. For the most part, our political candidates leave much to be desired. This manifests itself at several points in the overall political system.

In the first place, one only has to imagine oneself in the position of one of our first ministers trying to put together a cabinet. If he is lucky, he can draw upon a handful of competent individuals. After that, it is usually a question of who will cause the least damage or embarrassment.

The quality of many of our first ministers and their cabinets, as well as their counterparts in the other parties, helps to put the dilemma of the average voter in proper perspective. More often than not these days, the voter is voting more against a party or person than for a party or person. To many a voter, it is largely a matter of selecting those likely to do the least harm. This suggests that a "do nothing" party might do very well right now in this country.

The fact that so many people are exercising their franchise more negatively than positively helps to explain our low voter turnout. Often this is blamed on straight apathy when perhaps it should be attributed to disenchantment with the alternatives. One way to distinguish between the two would be to add another box to the ballot labeled succinctly "I Protest," or more fully, "The alternatives are too appalling for me to lend my support to any of them." If such a choice were added, it might just attract enough voters to persuade some party to try to appeal to the disillusioned element in the electorate.

Part of our current political malaise is also due to the seeming inability of our politicians to cope with so many of the problems which plague us or at least to explain their purported solutions in a satisfactory manner. An example of the latter phenomenon grows out of the worldwide energy crisis which has forced much higher prices on Canadians even though we were long led to believe that we were more than self-sufficient. While the government's policies may be very sensible in areas such as this, the public seems to have the feeling that we are helpless pawns in situations beyond our control.

Mention of the seeming inability of our politicians to keep on top of our energy crisis despite our supposed self-sufficiency in this area brings to mind those who charge that we have lost control over our entire economic destiny. Especially on the business or corporate side it is alleged that we have become a nation of truncated branch-plant operations run by multinational corporations over which we have little or no mastery. Our Foreign Investment Review Agency is considered a farce or fraud when it comes to effective control over foreign investment in this country. This could all become a somewhat moot question, of course, if we continue to choose to invest much more abroad than foreigners decide to invest here.

As if all this is not enough to lead to disenchantment about our politicians' ability and will to preside over us intelligently, there is the added concern provided by their propensity to generate massive deficits — particularly at the federal level. While attempting to grapple with our many problems, the federal government has undertaken expenditures which far exceed its revenues. This has led to a huge accumulation in our deficit which the government now seems only able to manage through large foreign borrowing. The cost of servicing this debt is now so great that it is approaching twenty percent of the total federal budget.

Last, but not least, is the disillusionment which has arisen in some quarters — not enough I'm afraid — because of the excesses of our security forces. The politicians seem to have little or no control over many of their activities. As a result, forces such as the RCMP apparently felt quite free to go about their business in a manner that violated civil liberties we had long taken for granted. Even when their excesses were revealed, some of our leaders demonstrated very little concern about the consequences which could ensue from this sort of unrestrained police behavior.

There are many other reasons why our political system is in so much difficulty. The blatant and cynical use of the Senate for patronage purposes is just one more example. All in all, it is really quite astounding that the public retains as much faith in our political processes as it does.

Continuing Stagflation. On the economic front, Canada's problems are aptly summarized by the term "stagflation." It embodies in one appropriate-sounding word the worst possible combination of circumstances — that is, slow or sluggish growth, high levels of unemployment, and persistent inflation.

As for real economic growth, Canada has been well below its potential for some years now. Our performance during the fifties and early sixties was above average due to the rapid rate of growth in our labor force and very favorable international terms of trade stemming from the premium on our resources. More recently, our growth has been quite dismal, not only in comparison with this earlier period, but also in relation to our potential. The most recent cause of this disappointing performance has been the general economic decline in the Western world. More domestic causes include our continuing shift from a goods-producing to a service-producing economy with its attendant loss in scope for productivity improvement. The rapid growth of government seems to have been especially significant in this context.

The slowdown in our growth rate helps to explain our continuing high levels of unemployment. Even in the best of times, Canada's unemployment tends to be higher than that of other developed countries because of our special regional, seasonal, and structural problems. But even these problems don't begin to explain our present levels of unemployment. Aside from sluggish growth, these levels of unemployment reflect the comparatively rapid rate of growth in our labor force, especially on the female side. Thus, in 1978, despite the creation of between 300,000 and 400,000 new part- and full-time jobs, unemployment was hardly reduced. It is conceivable that no real relief will come until the 1980s when the rate of labor force growth in this country is due to taper off.

Currently, both our growth rate and our unemployment level depend on several variables, only some of which are within our control. Much depends on a sustained recovery throughout the Western world. This, in turn, depends upon the ability of Germany, Japan, and the United States, in particular, to agree upon a mutually reinforcing and stimulating set of fiscal, monetary, and trade policies. In Canada, of course, we are especially vulnerable to what happens in the U.S. because of our extensive trading relations with our neighbor. Predictions are that the U.S. is heading into a mild recession which could become worse if it does not come up with more effective policies to deal with its fiscal deficits, its energy dependence, and its inflation problems.

As for inflation, matters seem to go from bad to worse. Despite an anti-inflation program entailing wage and price controls which was supposed to reduce inflation to four percent by 1978, it was over double that level in that year. Together with our unemployment record, this has given Canada one of the highest levels of economic discomfort in the Western world. This new economic discomfort index results from simply adding together the rate of unemployment and the rate of inflation. Canada may not lead in either area, but link them and we are hard to beat.

The inflation outlook depends on many domestic and foreign variables. As a major trading country, we are bound to be affected by the inflation rates of our leading trading partners. On the domestic front, our fiscal and monetary policies are critical. But it is also important to come to grips with some of the behavioral, institutional, and structural problems with which I will be dealing shortly.

I believe the challenge posed by inflation to be so central to the resolution of our many economic and social problems that I will reserve most of what I have to say on this subject for a separate chapter.

Living Beyond Our Means.   Another manifestation of our problems is our tendency to live beyond our means, both collectively and individually. Collectively, our tendency to live beyond our means has been reflected in our government's massive deficits. The federal government has been the worst offender ever since the mid-seventies. Ever since then it has been running up larger and larger deficits. These deficits were at first aggravated by similar deficits at the provincial level. More recently, led by Alberta with its Heritage Fund, the provinces in the aggregate have been operating with a substantial surplus.

The federal deficit is now constituted in part by what may be termed an "inflation deficit." This part of its deficit results from the fact that we have indexed both its inflow in the form of the income tax system and its outflow in the form of much of the social insurance system. We indexed the income tax system in order to prevent the government from benefiting from higher rates of taxes on our increased incomes, most of which were nominal due to inflation. We also indexed some of our social security payments to ensure that the recipients of such payments did not suffer from inflation. As laudable as each of these steps may have been in and of themselves, the effect was to reduce the intake of the federal treasury while at the same time increasing its payouts. This is the sense in which we now have an inflation deficit.

Individually, the best measure of our determination to live beyond our means has been the way in which our income advances have outstripped our productivity increases. This has not only normally been true in money terms but also occasionally in real terms. This demonstrates how successful we have been at extracting more from the system than it has proven capable of generating. It also helps to explain why, through our corporations, governments, and utilities, we have become so dependent on foreign sources of funds to finance our debts, deficits, and investments. As a result, our foreign indebtedness, both private and public, is becoming more and more burdensome.

Pricing Ourselves Out of World Markets. The net effect of many of the above trends has been a tendency to price ourselves out of world markets. One significant manifestation of this problem was the way in which our labor costs grew in relation to those of other countries. Labor costs grew so rapidly in this country for a time that among comparable countries, only Belgium and Sweden were in worse shape. Our incomes were growing disproportionately faster than those of other countries in comparison with our relative productivity performance.

To illustrate more dramatically our twin propensities to live beyond our means and price ourselves out of world markets one need only cite some recent Canadian-American comparisons. For a long time most Canadian wages and salaries lagged up to twenty percent behind their American equivalents, a difference almost identical with that of the productivity variation between the two countries. Then, for a time during the mid-seventies, wages and salaries rose about twice as fast as those in the United States. Before we knew it, many of our wages and salaries not only caught up to those of our American counterparts; they overtook them. Because there was no corresponding improvement in our overall productivity, something had to give.

The Decline in the Value of the Dollar. The Canadian dollar didn't fall almost twenty-five percent in relation to the U.S. dollar and about fifty percent in comparison to the German mark and the Swiss franc solely because we were pricing ourselves out of world markets. It also fell because of a new propensity among Canadians to invest more abroad while others chose to invest less here. Regardless of the combination of causes involved, the dramatic fall in the value of the Canadian dollar was as good a reminder as any that we were in serious difficulty.

Although indicative of our problems, the decline in the value of our dollar is also helping to resolve some of them by making our goods and services more competitive in both our domestic and foreign markets. Whether we retain this competitive advantage will depend more than anything else on our ability to keep inflation under control. Otherwise, we will dissipate the benefits accruing to us due to the lower dollar by driving up our costs.

Fortunately or unfortunately — depending on how one views the causes and effects — the dollar is likely to remain between eighty and ninety cents in terms of its U.S. equivalent for some time to come. This is fortunate because of the aforementioned effect on our trading position. It is unfortunate in the sense of increasing the burden of the large payouts we must bear in the form of both interest and dividends owed to foreigners, many of which are payable in American dollars. This is the price of our longtime dependence on foreign borrowing to finance what we have always been unwilling to finance ourselves. That this is unlikely to end for some time to come is borne out by the huge sums that our governments continue to draw on from abroad.

Another View of the Canadian Challenge

There is another threefold way in which to assess many of the problems confronting this country. These problems can be classified into three categories: behavioral, institutional, and structural.

Behaviorally, the point to be stressed is that no one group any longer accepts its position in the traditional income hierarchy or pecking order. There was never anything inherently just or right about that hierarchy or order, but at least it was accepted. That acceptance lent a great deal of stability to our system in the sense that everyone knew his relative place and was more or less willing to live with it.

All of this acceptance and stability has given way to a disquieting, new consensus in this country: now the only thing we all agree on is that everyone else is overpaid compared to us. It is this unsettling phenomenon as much as the rise in the cost of living which explains why we are in the midst of such a rat race. Everyone is determined to do better than everyone else in a frantic effort to improve his comparative position.

This general behavioral trend underscores the growing institutionalization of our society. To help improve their lot, more and more groups are resorting to collective organizations of one kind or another. Many of these institutions have been around for some time but have recently taken on renewed vigor. Take unions by way of illustration. While the union share of the labor force continues to shrink in the U.S., it is still growing in Canada. As a result, almost forty percent of the Canadian labor force is now organized, whereas the percentage has fallen to just over twenty percent south of the border.

But unions are not the only institutions which are thriving in the face of pressure to find a concerted means through which to pursue group ends. Various profession-al groups — doctors, lawyers, dentists, and so on — are now more overtly taking on the characteristics of unions. In the past they were more subtle about their ends and means, if only because the last thing they wanted to appear to be was a union. Now, even though they choose to call themselves associations or societies — anything but unions — it is more and more difficult for them to dis-guise what they really are. Indeed, in some ways, they make unions look like amateurs. After all, unions have always had to bargain with someone, whereas most professional groups usually just set their own fees without reference to anyone else. One might well term this pro-cess "collective bludgeoning" as opposed to collective bargaining.

Then, too, there are the farmers with their marketing boards. These boards are supposed to serve consumers as well as producers, but one has to wonder about their real priorities. Admittedly, quotas and other devices designed to regularize production can work to everyone's advan-tage. One has to query the result, however, when the most efficient producers are forced to operate at sub-optimum levels. The very fact that when votes are taken about the introduction of a marketing board the ballot is conducted solely among the producers affected indicates whose interests these boards are really intended to serve.

As for business and commerce, they have such a prolif-eration of national, regional, and local bodies to promote their objectives that one hardly knows where to start. From the largest corporate entities in this country, which often have enough clout on their own, to the smallest main-street storekeeper who belongs to the Canadian Federation of Independent Businessmen, business and commerce are well positioned to make sure their voices are both heard and heeded. Regulations, subsidies, and tariffs which have been introduced to advance and protect business interests in this country have increased steadily.

This brings me to the structural dimension of our challenge. While we have allowed the public sector to assume a much larger proportion of activities in this country, we have also chosen to protect large sections of the private sector from any real competition, either domestic or foreign. These trends cannot help detracting from our efficiency, inventiveness, and productivity. Just take the public sector alone. One of the most debilitating characteristics of government is that it is hard for it to go bankrupt. There is no bottom line and it cannot go out of business. Like a protected industry, it doesn't have to compete to survive. It thus lacks the incentive and motivation to do things as well as an enterprise whose very existence is on the line.

The plethora of regulations, subsidies, and tariffs are having a similar effect in the private sector. It is discouraging to discover how few businessmen truly believe in free enterprise. They all use the rhetoric, but few are prepared to live with the consequences. The ones who are, enjoy such a competitive advantage that they do not require any kind of assistance. Otherwise, they do not hesitate to ask for protective measures of one kind or another.

The Credibility of Our Institutions

Problems of confidence and credibility afflict virtually all our leading institutions. From week to week or month to month, it is largely a question of which of these institutions has most stretched the public's capacity for skepticism. It is almost as if these institutions were vying for the poorest image with the public.

Broadly speaking, we could now be confronted by a vicious circle of declining confidence and credibility. Although our political institutions may be in the forefront of this process, few institutions are free of it. In some ways, this trend is being fed by the lack of any fundamental commitment on our part to anything resembling equity, fairness, and justice. One important manifestation of this lack of concern is the breakdown in the traditional income hierarchy and pecking order. This is leading to further organization by all manner of groups to fight for a greater share of the current spoils and a better place in the wealth spectrum. The outcome is every conceivable form of juggling, leapfrogging, manipulating, seesawing, and whipsawing for position. We are on an inflationary treadmill to nowhere.

Given governments which are disposed to capitulate to almost every interest group and are unwilling to stand up to any but the weakest, it is no wonder that the public is losing faith in the whole process. Indeed, this basic weakness of governments adds to the confidence and credibility gap in a manner which turns it into a vicious circle. Once into that circle, it is hard for a society to break out, except in the case of a severe crisis or shock which threatens the very basis of the system, thereby forcing people to reassess what is ultimately at stake.

CHAPTER THREE

Making Politics a More Attractive Calling

IT IS NO accident that I should begin my prescriptive chapters by focusing on the need to make politics a more attractive calling. This is because our politicians are bound to have a much more telling effect on our future than many of us would wish. Virtually nothing else which I recommend makes any sense in the absence of politicians with the capacity and willingness to take the necessary remedial steps. It is a sad commentary that any such talents are more conspicuous for their absence than their presence on the current political scene.

The Caliber of Our Politicians

It is surprising that politics attracts even the few outstanding individuals it does, given a breakdown of the pros and cons of a political career in this country. But politics is far from attracting enough adequate and competent individuals, let alone outstanding ones.

At no point does this become more apparent than when we witness one of our first ministers attempting to build or rebuild his cabinet. During 1977 and 1978, it was pathetic to say the least to watch Trudeau and Davis try to improve upon their respective cabinets. In neither case were they able to do so, given the appalling weaknesses of their parties' backbenchers. Nor were their political opponents — the leaders of the opposition — in a position to have done any better.

Politics is simply not attracting the caliber of individual which it must if our governments and legislatures are to play the astute kinds of roles which they must in the years ahead. This is not hard to understand, given the life of the typical politician.

The Pros and Cons of a Political Career

If only to appear positive, one has to start with the appealing aspects of a career in politics. For many, if not most of those in politics, money is hardly the primary motivation. Many other careers are far more lucrative.

Rather, one must look to nonmonetary considerations. For some, I suppose, it is nothing more than an ego or power trip. Even the lowliest politician undoubtedly attracts far more attention in politics than he would in any other capacity. For others, it is the opportunity to influence the direction of events which is uppermost. For a few, it may be nothing more or less than the ennobling opportunity to serve their fellow men.

But the disadvantages of a political career would seem to outweigh the advantages. Already mentioned has been the financial disincentive. Most talented individuals can earn much more elsewhere. Again, however, moving away from the monetary side of the equation, there is the nature of the job itself. Many politicians have little or no private life. The demands placed upon them are immense. The higher they climb in the political world, the greater these demands become. No matter what level they reach, they must always contend with their constituents whose demands range from legitimate concerns to the pettiest grievances and gripes. It takes a lot of fortitude and patience to put up with this pressure.

In addition, there is the questionable status of politicians. Earlier, I cited ego gratification as one reason for entering politics. This suggests that the job carries more prestige than may actually be the case. Politicians as a whole do not enjoy the best reputations in our society. I recall an American survey which asked the public to rank the worthiness of twenty vocations, including that of the politician. The latter stood nineteenth in the ranking, to be outdone in lack of esteem only by the used car salesman. And this survey was taken before Nixon and Watergate.

None of this is to suggest that politics cannot pay off in many ways for those who are successful. Although the financial rewards may not be the greatest, the sense of power enjoyed by our first ministers and their leading colleagues is obviously very satisfying. Moreover, after you reach these exalted levels, the system seems to ensure that you do not suffer for the rest of your life. At the federal level, there is the Senate. At all levels, there are a variety of forms of patronage for those who have served the cause loyally. There is the bench; there are crown corporations, regulatory tribunals, and royal commissions. Moreover, if you have been a good Liberal or Tory, there are a host of company directorships and executive positions for those who have heeded the interests of the business establishment while serving in politics.

When all is said and done, however, the risks presently

associated with a political career are far too great for the average citizen to assume. For this reason alone, it is essential that many steps be taken to make politics a more attractive calling.

Higher Salaries

I hesitate to start with the matter of salaries because the thought of anyone making a good living in politics seems to upset many people. I find this point of view difficult to accept for two primary reasons. First, particularly at the federal and provincial levels, I can think of no more demanding or important positions than those held by our MPs and MPPs in terms of our society's future well-being. Second, we live in a society in which money remains the primary incentive and motivation. If one accepts my first premise about the critical role of the politician, then it follows that they should be among the highest paid in our society.

With these two considerations in mind, I do not hesitate to advocate a salary of $100,000 for our federal members of Parliament. Nor would I shy away from something approaching that amount for the members of our provincial legislatures in the larger provinces. To put that amount in perspective, let me point out that many corporate executives are paid as much. So are many athletes and entertainers. Even pilots on large jets have salaries approaching that figure.

The idea of indexing such a high salary in relation to the cost of living could prove even more controversial than the salary itself. Yet despite many misgivings and reservations about the notion of indexing any income, I would make an exception in this one case. I would make this exception to try to remove the matter of salaries from the political arena for the foreseeable future. In part, this reflects the revulsion I experience when politicians at any level vote themselves increases in their remuneration while they are in office. No such increase should ever come into effect without the electorate having a chance to choose between the better candidates such an increase is supposed to attract.

To indicate how serious I am about the latter point, let me suggest how I would move toward a $100,000 salary for our federal members of Parliament. Needless to say, I would not introduce it overnight. Rather, I would phase it in over two or three elections. Thus, the salary might rise to $50,000 after the next election; to $75,000 after the next one; and to the full $100,000 only after still another election. That would give the system ample time to attract better caliber candidates. While an increase might also attract some fast-buck artists, the electorate would presumably catch up to them if they weren't doing an effective job.

As for expenses and other forms of income, let me only make a couple of points. Without attaching an amount to it, I would allow our federal members of Parliament at least enough expense money to maintain an adequate constituency office and a small research and secretarial staff in Ottawa. I would also continue to make free transportation available to MPs traveling to and from their ridings.

The matter of outside income poses a dilemma. At the very least, I would compel every MP and MPP to disclose fully all of his outside interests. Beyond that requirement I am not sure that I would restrict them at all. As long as their constituents have ready access to all their sources of outside income, it is not clear to me what form an even and fair restriction could take. I would hope that any politician would abstain from voting on any matter in which he had a direct or significant indirect interest, but I would leave that matter to his conscience or, failing that, to the judgment of his constituents.

In calling for such high remuneration for our MPs, I realize that I will be accused of wanting to create a new, elite breed of politician. There is a risk of that, at least in the sense of such well-paid individuals losing touch with the common man. I discount that risk simply because a politician's constituents would soon dispense with any such individual. More important to me is the need to attract a wider range of talent to our high electoral offices — something which I deem to be impossible without much more attractive remuneration.

Leaves of Absence

Higher salaries alone will not attract more capable candidates to public office. Many other considerations are involved, not the least of which should be a leave of absence from one's normal employment. Both the jobs and the income increases to which successful candidates would normally have been entitled should be protected as long as they are serving in any full-time political office. By law, furthermore, candidates for such office should be entitled to a leave of absence without pay during an election campaign.

Right now, just about the only group in society which enjoys these advantages is the legal profession. This is perhaps the major reason why that profession is so disproportionately represented at all levels of politics in this country. Every major law firm wants to have at least one ex-MP or MPP and one Senator represented on its letter-head. If nothing else, it helps ensure a share of the legal patronage which all governments have available to dispense to their friends. It may even help them acquire a few more QCs and some of the waning prestige which still accrues to that blemished honor. Moreover, the legal profession as a whole cannot help benefiting from the legal knots their colleagues tie the rest of us in while they are in our legislatures. In a very real sense, the latter can be described as little more than make-work projects for that honorable profession.

My own employer, the University of Toronto, has a comparatively generous leave policy for aspiring and successful politicians within its ranks. In effect, we are entitled to paid leave for four weeks prior to an election and unpaid leave for up to five years as long as we serve as an MP or MPP. Yet even this policy has flaws, other than its five-year limit. One's leave is canceled if one ever becomes a cabinet minister or leader of the opposition. In other words, one is cut adrift if one ever reaches a posi-tion in politics where he can really accomplish something. It's almost as if the university is saying, "Don't become too relevant or useful, or we won't take you back!"

Two other points about a leave of absence for those elected to public office. The first is simply a reminder that during wartime we have adopted such a policy for those serving in the armed services. Surely our elected politi-cians are just as important to our long-term well-being in peacetime as our troops are during wartime. The second point is that anyone serving in high public office is almost certain to be worth more to his employer when he returns from such an experience. Only in the case of relatively small employers, therefore, when the inconvenience involved could be very serious, should any exception be made to the principle of leaves of absence.

Party Lists and Cabinet Ministers

The idea of party lists will resurface several times during the course of this volume. For the moment, it will suffice to indicate that these party lists would be composed of the names of prominent figures selected by their party to be elected on the basis of proportional representation. They would be added to those members of the legislature still elected on a constituency basis. Those on the party lists would not run at the individual constituency level but rather would campaign on a national basis along with the party leaders. Presumably, most of those on each party's list would be cabinet ministers or prospective cabinet ministers.

In the present context, the purpose of this proposal would be to free some key individuals in each party from the trials and tribulations of local constituency politics. This would allow them to concentrate on broader national issues within their spheres of competence. Cabinet ministers or aspiring cabinet ministers have enough to think about in terms of their present or prospective portfolios without having to concern themselves with the day-to-day concerns of local constituents. Party lists could serve as another means to attract and free more potential talent at the critical ministerial level. Neither higher salaries nor leaves of absence nor both together might be enough to satisfy this crying need.

The Legislature and Its Members

Trying to attract a higher caliber of member to our legislatures could prove a futile effort if the legislative process remains as meaningless as is now the case. Such individuals would become so bored and frustrated by the whole experience that they would either quit in mid-stream or not seek re-election.

Since much will be said about legislative reform later on, what is said at this point should be taken as little more than an introduction to what is to follow. Basic to any reform of our legislatures must be a revitalized committee structure featuring ample legal, research, and secretarial staff for the opposition side of such committees as well as the government. So restructured, many of these committees could not only do a better job of reviewing proposed legislation, but could also assume the job of so many recent royal commissions. The existence of so many royal commissions reflects the weakness of our present legislative committees as much as anything else.

The essential need is to make the role of the back-bencher more rewarding and satisfying, not to mention useful. Otherwise, no amount of enticement will lead talented people in our society to commit themselves for any length of time to that role.

A Code of Ethics for Parliamentarians

Earlier it was suggested that no limits should be placed on our Parliamentarians' outside sources of income, but that they should be compelled to disclose all such sources of income and the amounts involved. A few other requirements are probably indispensable if our Parliamentarians are to rise above the many conflicts of interest to which they can become party.

Among other things, our Parliamentarians should be barred from accepting any contracts with government, from lobbying for a fee on behalf of any group, or from benefiting from, or disclosing, inside information. Similar restrictions should undoubtedly also apply to those serving in the public service and its offshoots.

In the case of our Parliamentarians, the point is to dissuade those few unscrupulous individuals who might be tempted to take undue advantage of their positions of public trust to the detriment of both their high office and those serving with them.

CHAPTER FOUR

A Bill of Rights for Canadians

CANADIANS SHOULD HAVE an entrenched bill of rights as part of any new constitution we adopt. Such a bill of rights is not only required to protect us from each other; it is required to protect us from our governments. The power of the state can be awesome, whether it is democratically constituted or otherwise. The tyranny of the democratic majority can be just as frightening as that of a dictatorship.

Basic Individual Rights

A bill of rights for all Canadians could cover any number of rights. For our collective protection, for example, one could include under such a bill all rights associated with free elections, the electoral process itself, and access to the legislature. These are obviously fundamental rights which should be included in our constitution, although not necessarily as part of a bill of rights. In a bill of rights, we might be better advised to concentrate on the more individual aspects of our civil liberties.

The problem is that no individual rights can be completely absolute in a free society since one man's rights can so easily infringe upon another's. Nonetheless, there are a series of rights which can almost be ranked in order of their priority. As an academic and as a contributor to the media, I would be inclined to place freedom of expression and opinion at the top of the list. Others might give priority to freedom of conscience, religion, and thought. Still others might stress freedom of association and assembly, which I again deem especially important because of my background in industrial relations.

These rights are all so basic that one would like to think of them as being almost absolute. Yet even they cannot be granted such an exalted status. Freedom of expression and opinion, for example, cannot be treated as an absolute lest it lead to libel or incite to violence. Nor should the right of association and assembly be permitted at the expense of the individual rights of others affected by these rights.

Not mentioned thus far is the need for a constitutional provision barring discrimination based on race, creed, color, religion, or sex. Even in this area, absolutes are no doubt impossible, although any exceptions allowed should surely be few and far between.

The relative nature of individual rights becomes even more obvious when we move to others which would probably have to be qualified even in a bill of rights. Among such rights, I would include freedom of contract and freedom of property. Obviously, contracts designed to serve an illegal purpose or which exploit weaker groups in our society — such as minors — should not be sacrosanct. Nonetheless, as in the case of property rights, the right to contract should be recognized as an important one. Just as no one's property should be confiscated or expropriated without proper cause and compensation, no one's contractual rights should be jeopardized unless there are good and valid reasons.

Even more controversial would be the inclusion of the right to strike or lock out in a bill of rights. Since industrial conflict can jeopardize the health, safety, or well-being of the public, no such right could be included in the absence of a recognition that society, through the legislature could remove or suspend it where grievous harm is being done to the body politic. Despite the interpretative difficulties this would present, I would favor a positive, though qualified, declaration within our constitution supporting the right to strike or lock out. If nothing else, such a declaration might discourage our legislatures from moving prematurely and unnecessarily to terminate strikes and lockouts.

Other contentious matters include the question of equality of opportunity and freedom from human degradation, poverty, and suffering. Perhaps matters such as these have no place in a bill of rights. One then is left wondering where they do belong. Our society is supposedly based on the premise of equality of opportunity; yet our batting average in this critical area is low. More universal education and medicare have moved us in the direction of equality of opportunity. But the gradual removal of inheritance taxes in this country, while no doubt desirable for some economic reasons, is a most retrograde step for a society committed to equality of opportunity.

As for freedom from human degradation, poverty, and suffering, we have come a long way compared to many other countries. And yet, many disadvantaged persons continue to live in a deprived state in our rural and urban areas. One can hardly argue that their children enjoy anything like equality of opportunity, let alone a decent standard of living. Their lot might not seem as appalling were it not for the extremes at the other ends of the income and wealth spectrums. But these matters raise such fractious social issues that it is doubtful whether our constitution could even contain a commitment to the principles involved.

Reverting back to three somewhat less debatable issues, there are the questions of language rights, privacy, and freedom of information. Language rights are so basic to this country's future that they merit a separate section, both in our constitution, and in this work. So also does the matter of freedom of information, especially as it pertains to government secrecy. The issue of privacy is nowhere dealt with separately but pervades several parts of this chapter and particularly the section on private rights and public security.

Whatever basic individual rights are enshrined in our constitution, they must be accompanied by a commitment to what is known as "due process" and "the rule of law" to give them any meaning. Beyond these fundamental legal concepts, there must be adequate mechanisms ensuring the protection of individual rights. While some individuals are in a position to see to the protection of their rights on their own, the majority of Canada's citizens are not. Many private and public instruments are doubtless required to look to the defense of their rights as well as those of the rest of us. The role of federal and provincial human rights commissions, legal aid schemes, and ombudsmen come immediately to mind. So does the work of the Canadian Civil Liberties Association. Vigilance on the part of these and other groups will be essential to protect our civil liberties, even if they are eventually incorporated into our constitution.

The Case for Constitutional Protection

I find the arguments against entrenching fundamental human rights within our constitution hard to accept. Those who oppose such constitutional guarantees emphasize the need for governmental and legislative flexibility and freedom in order to cope with a rapidly changing society. This argument would seem to have some merit in the case of the more controversial rights mentioned in the last section, such as freedom from human degradation, poverty, and suffering. But it hardly applies to the basic rights such as freedom of speech.

Some opponents also seem to believe that our courts might be less vigilant in defending our civil liberties than would be our legislatures. Given the track record of some of our legislatures, this hardly seems plausible. But as in the case of the first objection to constitutional safeguards, it is to be stressed that they would not be tablets of stone. If the basic rights spelled out in the constitution become obsolete, or if the courts appeared to be misinterpreting them, these deficiencies could be remedied by a constitutional amendment.

More than offsetting these objections to a constitutional bill of rights is the strong case to be made for one. The main argument for such a bill is to be found in the aforementioned track record of our governments and legislatures. Both historically and more recently, they have condoned if not actually encouraged, all manner of violations of civil liberties. One need only cite our confinement of Japanese Canadians on the West Coast during World War II or the Duplessis regime's infamous record of violating civil liberties with its antilabor and antipress padlock laws and the like. More recently, there was the federal government's abuse of the War Measures Act in Québec. Now Québec wants its own version of such an act innocently entitled "An Act Respecting the Protection of Persons and Property in the Event of Disaster." Revelations about the activities of the RCMP — about which more will be said later — are enough in themselves to persuade me of the need for something more than the limited federal statutory bill of rights we now have.

Beyond the track record of particular governments and legislatures in this country, there is the fact that we have eleven different sets of them at the federal and provincial levels alone. We are unlikely to have a very even incidence of civil liberties in this country in the absence of an overriding constitutional bill of rights which applies to all our governments.

There is one modified approach to a constitutional bill of rights which might make sense without giving either the judiciary or the legislatures exclusive control over the matter. The Supreme Court could be empowered to render any law or regulation inoperative, though not unconstitutional, if it were deemed to infringe unduly on individual liberties. Then the legislature in question would have to reenact the offending law or regulation—something it would probably not do without due regard for the court's opinion.

However we choose to protect basic civil rights in this country, the point to be stressed is that they are too fundamental to be left strictly to the vagaries of governments and legislatures responding to the political winds of the day. The need to protect these liberties is too compelling to leave them solely to our elected representatives who can at times all too easily reflect the potential intolerance of the majority.

Bilingualism and Biculturalism

Much is made of the supposed bilingual and bicultural character of our nation. We even so titled one of our more famous royal commissions. To me, however, this represents one of the biggest hoaxes ever perpetrated on this country. It might be great if it were so — indeed, I think it would be — but it just isn't.

Essentially what we have in this country is a combination of colingualism and multiculturalism. We are increasingly colingual in the sense that Québec is becoming ever more exclusively French-speaking while virtually all of the rest of Canada remains essentially English-speaking. I think it is time that we faced up to the fact that we are a colingual, rather than a bilingual, nation.

What this means, in essence, is that if one chooses to live or work in Québec, one should be prepared to do so in French, while if one chooses to live or work elsewhere, one should be prepared to use English. By law or practice, only the capital district embracing Ottawa and Hull should be treated as a fully bilingual area.

This is not to deny that we should strive to bilingualize appropriate parts of the federal service outside the capital district. Nor is it meant to discourage the teaching of the second official language in as many of our schools as possible. It is merely to acknowledge that it is unrealistic to expect that every province will make bilingual services available on a general basis. At a minimum, however, there should be at least one central office in every province where information and some basic services are made available in the second language. Similarly, in terms of the courts, there should probably be one bilingual court in each of the provinces. Beyond these minimal requirements, however, public resistance is likely to be encountered if only because of the costs involved. It is really impractical to go any further.

As for the question of biculturalism, this too is a misnomer. But instead of coculturalism, the appropriate term in this case is multiculturalism. We tend to exaggerate the multicultural character of our country, but it is appealing to think of something other than the American melting pot. Having said this, there is still no doubt that there are two basic cultures in this country — one distinctly French-Canadian, the other at its best something called English-Canadian and, at its worst, called plain ordinary American. Within both cultures there has been a third dimension added by the many ethnic groups which have immigrated to Canada. They have made a great contribution to this country, not the least of which is a cultural one.

Neither on the linguistic nor the cultural side is it easy to decide what, if anything, should be said about multiculturalism in our constitution. Perhaps nothing should be said about it unless some sort of general preamble is thought useful. In that event, a general endorsement of our multicultural mosaic might well be included. On the language front, I would reject any constitutional commitment to bilingualism, except in the relatively narrow sense I have already outlined. Rather, I would place the emphasis on what I have termed colingualism, making it clear that there were and remain two major languages in the country — one confined largely to Québec and the other to the remainder of the provinces.

Private Rights and Public Security

Basic civil liberties are most likely to be threatened in the name of maintaining public security. This becomes obvious whether one considers the preservation of law and order in society on a daily basis or the protection of the country's national security. I find it difficult myself in many instances to reconcile the potential clash between private rights and public security.

Let me start with some cases where I find myself at odds with my civil libertarian friends. There is continuing controversy today about the right of a police officer to ask for a citizen's identification whether or not he is suspected of a crime. I do not believe it is an undue infringement of individual rights to expect one to have to comply with such a request. There is another controversy over whether or not the owner of an automobile should be required to identify who was driving it if it is suspected of being involved in an accident. Otherwise, some feel the owner should be held responsible. Again, I do not find this an undue infringement of individual rights. In these types of cases, I find myself sympathetic with the police who would otherwise be hard-pressed to enforce many reasonable laws in this country.

It is quite another matter when it comes to such measures as letter opening, telephone tapping, and search and/or seizure. In almost all such cases, I would require that the police seek a court order before they proceed and that such an order only be granted where the police can demonstrate substantial cause for such drastic actions. They do, after all, represent a tremendous invasion of the right of individual privacy. Only where the police have strong grounds for believing that a crime is in the process of being committed should anything less than a court order be required.

On the even more delicate question of national security, I again have mixed feelings. On the one hand, I feel that the RCMP must have some leeway in the protection of national security. Nonetheless, I am appalled at the lengths to which the RCMP have gone to serve the mandate which they felt they had in this area. It is bad enough that they burned barns, burglarized premises, and stole dynamite, among other nefarious activities. Yet these activities do not bother me as much as their close surveillance of a wide range of politicians and union leaders. This borders too closely on a police state, or a witchhunt designed to serve the party in power, to be comfortable. Clearly, the RCMP and our national security forces in general must be subject to more restraints than they have been in the past.

Whether these restraints can be handled by constitutional prohibitions is doubtful. The very nature of our security forces is such that they often have to operate in a clandestine fashion. This being the case, their overall supervision and day-to-day operation is critical. Nothing short of daily outside surveillance of all their activities would guarantee no abuse of their powers. Since this type of scrutiny is impossible and unrealistic, I would place my emphasis on the creation of an all-party committee along the British lines to oversee the entire national security operation.

Among the functions of such a committee would be the

promulgation of a code of conduct which all our security forces would be compelled to adhere to or face severe disciplinary action. Perhaps such a committee might even decide on the need for some kind of special appeal mechanism to which those in the lower ranks could turn for immediate advice and counsel on the legality of any orders about which they have serious misgivings or reservations. While such recourse would not protect them from later reprisals by their superior officers, it would at least protect them from punishment for exceeding their lawful authority.

Returning to the civilian sphere, I have equally strong feelings about public review boards within our police forces. I once proposed such a board for the Metropolitan Toronto Police Force with the police association nominating two members from outside their ranks, the editors of our leading newspapers naming two others, and the four together agreeing on a fifth member as chairman. Some variation of this proposal still makes sense to me with the board being empowered to hear appeals from aggrieved citizens about the conduct of the police. I would only empower the board to issue advisory opinions on the grounds that these should be enough in most cases and when insufficient would end up being dealt with at higher levels within the police and/or political hierarchies.

Freedom of Information

Last, but far from least, in terms of citizen rights within our country is the matter of freedom of information. For the moment, I will deal with this matter almost exclusively within the context of government itself. The fact that I feel equally strongly about access to hidden information in many of our private institutions will become clear later on.

It amazes me that a country as committed to democracy and freedom as we are supposed to be allows its governments to hide so much data from public view. Their undue secrecy cannot help making one suspicious about what they are hiding and why they are hiding it. The situation is so shameful in this country that Canadians must often go to the United States to uncover facts about their own country. Two recent cases involving the Securities Exchange Commission in the U.S., which is much more open about its work than any of its Canadian counterparts, will serve to exemplify this point.

In one case, a reporter resorted to the SEC in the United States to find out the salary of the president of Canadian Pacific. The president had refused to divulge the information and had bet the reporter that he could not find out. The other case involved Bell Canada's contentious contract with Saudi Arabia and the question of whether it required Bell to discriminate against present and prospective Jewish employees. Again, the data was found at the SEC in Washington. Because of its more comprehensive and open reporting requirements for any firm raising funds or selling stock in the United States, as Bell Canada does, it was willing to divulge the information.

Secrecy is an even greater problem within government itself. Aside from what transpires under its infamous Official Secrets Act, the federal government has so many categories and labels for its confidential materials that one hardly knows how to rank them. "Confidential,"

"For Cabinet Ministers Only," and "Top Secret" are three common labels. But my favorite has always been the one used by External Affairs: "For Canadian Eyes Only."

For two years I had fairly ready access to many of these materials. I was left with two enduring impressions. The first was the undue secrecy which prevailed. It was almost as if the authors of these materials felt no one would read them unless they were stamped "Classified." The second impression was of the low quality of much of the materials so labeled. It was shocking to think that anyone in government might act on the basis of some of the memoranda they were receiving which were not subject to any outside review. Perhaps it is fear of such outside scrutiny that really explains why the bureaucracy hides so much from public view.

In any event, we remain far behind the two model countries—Sweden and the United States—when it comes to freedom of information legislation. The former Liberal government employed everything from national security through ministerial responsibility and the cabinet requirement of secrecy to the need to protect the anonymity of civil servants to justify the withholding of all manner of information from the public. In one of the last versions of its so-called Freedom of Information Act about all that the government was willing to concede was that the public could see what the cabinet was willing to let it see. Thus, this act might have been better entitled a Freedom of Government Secrecy Act.

Since knowledge is power in government and politics as elsewhere, this situation cannot be tolerated. At the very least, a freedom of information act should embody a number of basic principles. The first of these is that any citizen or interest group should be entitled to ask for any information held by government. The government in question should have to produce that information within a specified time limit or give its reasons for refusing to do so. In the latter event, there should be an appeal mechanism — preferably to an information commissioner with the status of the auditor general — with the onus on the government to show why the information in question should not be released. Obviously, no information should be released in a manner which invades individual privacy.

The issue of freedom of information is so central and vital to the effective operation of liberal democracy that I would like to see a constitutional provision to the above effect. Then it would apply to all governments in Canada, thus bringing to an end their individual and even collective ability to operate behind closed doors and in secrecy for anything but a limited length of time.

CHAPTER FIVE

Federal-Provincial Relations

FEDERAL-PROVINCIAL RELATIONS represent the most complex and difficult aspect of the present constitutional crisis in Canada. This is because it is not easy to reconcile the conflicting economic and political pressures which are at work on the distribution of powers between our federal and provincial governments. On the one hand, there is a strong economic case to be made for more rather than less centralization of powers in Canada. On the other hand, there are even stronger political pressures pulling in the opposite direction.

Some Historical Perspectives

The BNA Act was clearly intended to ensure a strong central government within Confederation. To this end, the federal government was granted control over money and banking and trade and commerce within the list of specified powers and residual control over all unnamed powers. The major power granted to the provinces was over property and civil rights.

Despite the original intention of our founding fathers

and the British Parliament, the Judicial Committee of
the British Privy Council and later our own Supreme
Court chose greatly to expand the power of the provinces
at the expense of the central government. They did this
by narrowly interpreting the federal trade and commerce
clause and widely interpreting the provincial property
and civil rights clause.

It took the depression and World War II to reverse this
trend. After the depression, for example, the provinces
agreed to a constitutional amendment making unemployment insurance a federal responsibility. Then,
during World War II, the federal government virtually
took over the economy to further the war effort. One
result of this move was a wholesale transfer of the
important taxing powers to the federal government. This
set the stage for our postwar form of centrism based on
the federal government's rental of certain provincial
taxing powers, a proportion of the proceeds of which
were rebated to the provinces on the basis of a tax point
system. Ever since then, there has been an ongoing
struggle over this system.

Throughout this period the federal government has
used its tax authority under the rental agreements to steer
provincial spending in directions it favored. The two
major examples are in the fields of education and health
care where the federal government offered massive
financial incentives to induce the provinces to move
toward more universal post secondary education and
medicare. Now, however, as the federal government feels
compelled to reduce its spending, it is in a position to
withdraw its support from such programs, leaving the
provinces with the harsh choice of cutting back on them
or finding alternative sources of funding.

The continuing stuggle over the distribution of federal-provincial power and responsibilities began to heat up as the Quiet Revolution evolved in Québec. It was bad enough when the federal and provincial wings of the Liberal Party in Québec were at loggerheads. The situation has been greatly exacerbated since the Parti Québécois took over. Meanwhile, the new "have" provinces in the West, led by Alberta, began to assert themselves, especially in terms of their right to dispose of their resources as they saw fit.

Meanwhile, a seemingly more centrist-minded Supreme Court has been handing down a series of decisions suggesting a move away from its earlier position favoring provincial rights. Federally imposed wage and price controls were held to be constitutional, at least on a temporary basis, even though they represented a tremendous invasion of traditional areas of provincial rights, especially in the collective bargaining arena. Some provincial taxes on their resource industries were struck down, if only in the form in which they were initially imposed. It was also made clear that federal marketing boards took priority over their provincial counterparts.

It is against this general background that one has to assess the current battle over federal-provincial relations in this country. It is paramount to begin any such assessment by weighing the prospects for Québec's separation since this possibility obviously represents the most extreme threat to the status quo.

Québec and Separation

The roots of the separatist cause in Québec run very deep indeed. Many Québecois feel they have always been a subjugated people. They began as a French colony only to become an English colony. Then, when Canada gained its independence, they became a minority within the new Confederation. Later on, they came to feel they were subordinate to a combination of English-Canadian and U.S. influences.

The most disquieting manifestation of this feeling of inferiority was to be found in the economic sphere. *Les Anglais* dominated the employer class, whereas the Québecois provided the labor. It does not matter today that these roles were partly, if not largely, to be explained by the highest form of subjugation to which the Québecois were ever prone. As noted earlier, it was their own Catholic Church which denied them access to the skills required in business and commerce. Rather, even the sons and daughters of the more privileged Québecois were confined to a classical education and pointed in the direction of the clergy, law, or medicine.

However it came to pass, the Québecois came to feel economically disadvantaged within their own province. The working language of those who succeeded in business and commerce was English, and those without a facility in that language could afford only limited aspirations. When the education system broke out of its previously narrow Catholic or classical mold and began to provide French Canadians with the capacity to do well within a more modern industrial world, something had to give.

The ball of change was already rolling when the Liberal Party, under Jean Lesage, embarked on the Quiet Revolution. Any inferiority complex that remained gave way to pride in everything French-Canadian. The Québecois language and culture gradually became something to be cherished and championed instead of being sacrificed to the altar of success, North American style. Hydro-Québec was formed as if to demonstrate that Québec could do its own thing in the business and commercial sphere. Expo was held to trumpet the new French-Canadian image as much as that of Canada as a whole. Despite the pace of these changes, they did not involve any sort of rude awakening for the rest of Canada.

All this was to change very quickly when René Lévesque and the Parti Québécois came to power. They succeeded primarily because of their welcome condemnation of the incompetence of the previous Liberal administration. Indeed, they played down their separatist aspirations until after they were elected. Since then, they have dedicated themselves to that end, although in its supposedly new, watered-down form termed "sovereignty-association." However described, their goal is clearly an independent Québec with whatever relations it voluntarily chooses thereafter to have with the rest of Canada.

As part of its long-run separatist strategy, the PQ is now striving for a referendum with wording so fuzzy that it cannot help carrying. What it really wants is a resolution along the lines of California's Proposition 13, which few could resist without undercutting their self-interest in whatever kind of Québec they favor. Thus, the referendum may request no more than public backing of the Québec government in its attempt to negotiate a better deal with Ottawa for Québec and its citizens. Even if a much more hard-line question were asked in the referendum, it might carry more votes than English Canada assumes. I would bet on about a thirty to forty percent vote, even if the referendum called for total separation from the rest of Canada.

Whatever happens, the issue of separation is not going to fade away quickly in Québec. Even if both the PQ and its referendum go down to defeat, a significant minority of Québecois will continue to press for eventual separation. Moreover, they might prove easier to deal with than Claude Ryan, the new leader of the Québec Liberal Party, who is looked upon as a solid federalist. Because of this stance, it will be hard to resist his demands if he is ever elected premier of the province, since he will claim to be speaking in the name of a united Canada.

What impresses me about the separatist cause is its strong base among academics, entertainers, members of the media, and trade union leaders. Together, these elements represent a potent and powerful force in any society. Moreover, they can almost make their objective a self-fulfilling prophecy. By keeping the pot boiling, they add to the uncertainty which is discouraging investment in the province, thereby exacerbating the obvious disparities which already exist between Ontario and Québec. Thus Confederation is made to look like a bad deal. Because of these considerations, separation is not likely to diminish as a real threat to Canada for some time to come.

Although special status for Québec appears to be unpalatable to most English Canadians, nothing short of this is ever likely to resolve the problem. Québec already enjoys such a status in terms of its civil code. Its increasingly unilingual character also sets it apart from the rest of the country. To me, the only question really worth considering is what additional forms this special status must assume.

In contemplating this question, I am reminded of the debate which took place some years ago within the Canadian Labour Congress concerning the status of the Québec Federation of Labour, its wing in that province. In the end, the CLC had no choice but to grant the QFL special status because of the different milieu in which it was operating. At the time, I remember contemplating how much the CLC reflected Canadian society in general when it was wrestling with this challenge.

Just as the CLC was concerned about how far it should go in granting the QFL special status, so the rest of Canada has every right to be concerned about how much it should concede to Québec. Obviously, there is a point beyond which such concessions would really amount to *de facto* separation. There is no question about cultural and linguistic matters. Nor need one get too upset over education, health, and many other social matters. But when it comes to basic fiscal, monetary, and trade matters, even the most liberal English Canadians are likely to balk.

I can only hope that the majority of Québecois will not push the rest of Canada to the breaking point. They already know that they can secure most of what they need to preserve their own language and culture within Confederation. Moreover, there are economic risks in separatism. All Canada will suffer economically if Québec separates, and it is difficult to discern whether Québec would suffer more or less than the rest of the country. If nothing else, Québec should bear in mind its highly vulnerable textile industry and its relatively dependent state in terms of some vital sources of energy.

Not to be minimized on the noneconomic side is the kind of nationalism which Québec could come to embody. Although it may be too strong to suggest that Québec nationalism could take a bigoted and racist form, it could prove very narrow and negative in character. One need only cite the proposed laws calling for government licensing of all bookstores in Québec to see that their nationalism could easily become very authoritarian.

The one point I would stress above all others is that if we fail to find a mutually satisfactory compromise, we must allow Québec to decide on its own future course. I believe Québec would be foolish to go its own way, but I believe even more strongly that it must have the right to make such a tragic mistake. I take this position even though I am certain that it would eventually prove fatal to the survival of both English Canada and Québec.

Alberta and the Other Resource Provinces

Québec is far from the only threat to the unity of this country. Indeed, at times Alberta appears to be an even greater menace to Confederation. At least, Québec can claim to fear for the loss of its original culture and language. All Alberta seems to care about is control over its resources. And it has allies. Saskatchewan shares many of Alberta's views in light of its vast potash and uranium resources, and British Columbia is also very conscious of its basic wealth in raw materials. Even the Maritimes are showing more sympathy for Alberta's position because of the much improved prospects for their fisheries due to the new 200-mile limit. If oil and gas are found off the East Coast, the priorities of the East and West could become one.

In the end, this could leave Ontario as the only province favoring a strong federal government. Ontario's position is hardly surprising since this has been its stand ever since the national policy made it the chief benefactor of Canadian industrialization. Now that its favored position is on the line, it is bound to be the most reticent about any changes in the existing federal-provincial distribution of powers.

Assuming the provinces are granted greater control over economic matters and particularly over their resources, the potential scope for income differentials between the various provinces and regions could widen. One need only think of the rapidity with which Alberta's Heritage Fund is building up, despite cutbacks in the province's taxes and increases in its spending, to appreciate the magnitude of the discrepancies which are emerging between our provinces and regions. This trend will have to be accompanied by a renewed commitment to our present system of equalization payments if it is not to put to the test the very existence of this country.

The Costs of Decentralization

The costs of decentralization are so many and varied that they are hard to list, let alone rank in order of importance. What follows, however, is a brief resumé of the perils we face if this country becomes more divided and fragmented than it is already.

Certainly, the fiscal and monetary management of the country will become more difficult if provincial spending and taxing powers are enlarged at the expense of the federal government. The problems involved in trying to coordinate the fiscal policies of one federal and ten provincial governments are already immense. The costs of a continuing failure to do so will be even more telling if the federal share in the system is further diminished. I would press this argument even more forcefully if the federal government had not handled its fiscal management of the economy so poorly over the last ten years or so. Its performance has been so negligent that we might have been, and perhaps could still be, better off if it carried less weight in the overall system.

Just as worrisome as the fiscal and monetary management of the economy in a more decentralized federal-provincial framework is the increasing balkanization of the country for trade purposes. This country makes little enough sense as a viable economic unit when it is taken as a whole. The situation is made more severe by provincial attempts to build barriers around themselves. "Buy provincial" campaigns and requirements are probably the greatest menace in this area. But they are not the only ones. Provinces can also manipulate all manner of regulations, standards, and subsidies to favor provincial as opposed to out-of-province enterprises. All of this only serves to carve up the already-limited Canadian market to a point where producers are denied the volume necessary for economies of scale sufficient to make them competitive internationally, if not domestically as well.

Another cost of further decentralization of government power in Canada is bound to show up on the social side. Through a system of equalization payments, this country has attempted with some success to iron out the greatest income disparities between its various provinces and regions. Through these payments, revenues are, in effect, simply transferred from our wealthiest areas to our poorest ones. It is hard to believe that such a system would survive in the absence of a strong federal presence.

Some Basic Premises

Despite the costs involved, this already decentralized Confederation of ours will probably have to become even more decentralized if it is to survive. The political pressures working for such decentralization are just too strong to resist. This being the case, what I would concentrate on are some fundamental principles which we must hold inviolate if we are to be left with anything workable.

Although this may seem to contradict some of the things I have just said, the other provinces are going to have to accept Québec's separate status if we are to work things out. Because of its distinct language and culture, there is a strong case to be made for such status. If all the other provinces insist on similar concessions, however, it will probably tear Canada apart.

Apropos of what I have already said about equalization payments, these must be accepted as a fundamental part of any new Confederation pact. Indeed, I would argue that they are so vital that at least the principle involved should be enshrined in the constitution. How far we could or should go beyond such a basic constitutional commitment is debatable.

A third prerequisite pertains to the provincial balkanization of our national markets. If this country cannot even preserve its limited national markets, any economic rationale for its continuation will fade into the background. Both our competitive position and our standard of living would be jeopardized.

Finally, I would stress the need for more effective coordination of federal and provincial policies both in the fiscal and monetary spheres and elsewhere. Perhaps such coordination can be brought about through the plethora of federal-provincial and interprovincial bodies that already exist, but this seems unlikely, given the record on this score to date. At the very least, we must strive to make our first ministers' meetings and their innumerable subcommittees and other spinoff groups much more meaningful undertakings.

CHAPTER SIX

The Parliament of Canada

THIS CHAPTER FOCUSES on the House of Commons as if it were the only part of our Parliament. This presupposes the abolition of the Senate which I have long favored for reasons set out in the next chapter. Failing abolition, the Senate must be subject to such drastic surgery that in the end it will bear little resemblance to its present form.

With or without a Senate, the House of Commons must be our preeminent national legislative assembly. To play this role more effectively than it has in the past, the House of Commons must be reformed in a number of ways, some of which have already been dealt with in Chapter Three. Assuming abolition of the Senate, I would begin by renaming the present House of Commons the Parliament of Canada. Although this might only seem to amount to a cosmetic and superficial change, it would be an effective way to signify a new start.

The Present House of Commons

Many problems afflict the present House of Commons besides the discouragingly low caliber of so many of its

members. Some thoughts on how this depressing characteristic can be alleviated have already been offered. Some
of the points brought out in this chapter should also help
correct this situation.

Perhaps the most worrisome feature of the present
House of Commons is how meaningless it is as a legislative chamber. In large part, this is a manifestation of
the limited role it plays in policy formulation. This, in
turn, reflects a number of considerations including the
weakness of its committees, the role of party discipline,
and the almost complete absence of free votes.

At no times does the House of Commons appear more
pathetic than when it is dealing with the budget. Because
the budget is surrounded by an unnecessarily high degree
of secrecy, it is presented to the House virtually as a *fait
accompli*. Seldom is it given proper committee study or
debated very intelligently. Instead, the House, in effect,
becomes a rubber stamp. There is a kind of ritual dance
associated with the process, but that is about all. The
majority party is already precommitted to it while the
opposition is preordained to oppose it.

As in the case of the budget, the problem in so many
other areas is that the House as a whole cannot do justice
to the complexity of the issues involved. This is why the
committee structure of the House is so critical. Only with
effective committees can proper scrutiny be given to most
bills coming before the House. Yet this is where the House
of Commons normally fails completely to do its job.
Compared to the U.S. Congressional Committees, those
of the Canadian House of Commons come close to being
a farce. They lack the resources and staff to begin to do a
competent job. Worse still, all too often those sitting on
the committees function solely as partisan members of

their party rather than as individuals trying to work out reasonable solutions to obvious problems.

Two recent exceptions to this general rule involved the Parliamentary Committee on Penal Reform and the Special Joint Committee on Immigration. In both cases neither the government nor the opposition parties had any fixed views on what should be done and were willing to allow the committees to try to work out some solutions on a nonpartisan basis. It is unfortunate that these welcome precedents have not been followed in other areas.

Party discipline is the central issue in the challenge of making the House more effective. Party discipline is basic to the parliamentary system of government which, on balance, remains superior to the congressional form of government. At least, the parliamentary system ensures that a party or group of parties is responsible for running the government. Offsetting the advantages of the party discipline which makes this possible is the stultifying effect it has on the individuals who are subjected to it. Although they are free to speak their minds in their party caucuses, outside them they resemble braying donkeys or flapping seals more than thinking individuals.

One way to get around this dilemma would be to have more free votes. There are clearly many matters on which a government must be able to call upon its members to rally to its side, regardless of their personal feelings. But there are many other matters on which free votes could be called so that members could vote according to their consciences. There would have to be an interparty agreement on such votes, and they could not be treated as votes of confidence in the government. In other words, the government would not necessarily fall on the basis of such votes.

A New Parliament of Canada

One cannot help describing how a new Parliament of Canada should function in the course of reviewing how the present House of Commons has been performing. Nevertheless, it is important to enlarge on some of the points just made as well as some others.

In Chapter Three, the importance of party lists was discussed as one means of attracting more qualified people into politics. I explained at that time that these lists would be composed of the names of prominent individuals selected by their parties and that these individuals would not run at the constituency level, but would campaign on a national basis along with the party leaders. It is now time to clarify how these party lists would fit into the overall parliamentary setup.

First, they would mean an enlargement of the House since its present basis of individual constituency members would be retained. No fewer than fifty and perhaps as many as one hundred new seats would be added to the new Parliament, all to be based on the regional proportional vote achieved by any party securing at least ten percent of that vote. Each party would place on its regional lists in order of their priority its leading candidates for the cabinet or the shadow cabinet. Such individuals would presumably be selected with due regard for the English-French and other regional characteristics of the country. Nonetheless, they would be running nationally and, therefore, they would probably campaign more on national than local or constituency issues.

The most important result to be achieved by such an approach would be to ensure that the major national parties had representatives from across the country — even where they could not secure such representation purely on the basis of the results in individual constituencies. Thus, the Conservatives could command a more legitimate and meaningful contingent from Québec while the Liberals would benefit from a similar result in the West. Even the NDP would become a more truly national party on the basis of such a formula.

In terms of the day-to-day functioning of a new Parliament of Canada, tremendous emphasis would have to be placed on the work of its committees. Here, as already suggested, I would not hesitate to adopt the American Congressional Committee model even though ours is a parliamentary system. I find no fundamental conflict between the two in this context. Both the majority and the minority party members on each committee should have legal counsel, research staff, and secretarial personnel commensurate with the work load of the committee in question. The committees should be free to initiate investigations into areas within their jurisdiction on their own. More important, however, no legislation within their sphere of competence should pass Parliament before they have had adequate time to review it. At the very least, this would mean enough time to hold hearings before which all manner of interested parties could appear to make their views known.

The committees should also be free to summon witnesses and subpeona evidence germane to any matter before them. Needless to say, the minister sponsoring any bill would be expected to introduce it before the committee and to reappear from time to time as required by the committee to explain and enlarge upon it.

The case for more free votes in Parliament was made in the previous section. Together with the other changes recommended here, as well as elsewhere in this volume, this reform would help to turn Parliament into a much more vibrant and vital institution. Nothing less will do if it is to attract a higher caliber of individual and to assume its rightful place in the Canadian political process.

CHAPTER SEVEN

The Senate: Abolition or Reform

THE EFFICACY OF the Canadian Senate has long been debated. I have already made my own position clear. I would abolish it. Only if that proves impossible — as it long has — would I consider reform. Any such reform will obviously have to be drastic if it is to do any good. At the very least some way must be found to avoid the Senate's present use as a kind of burial or dumping ground for party bagmen and has-been politicians. Beyond this prerequisite, there is the question of whether the Senate should be turned into a legislative review chamber more reflective of provincial and regional interests.

The Case for Abolition of the Senate

The case for abolition of the Senate rests on two primary grounds. The first concerns the issue of whether a second chamber is really necessary. The second concerns the likelihood of the Senate being used as anything other than the aforementioned burial or dumping grounds for loyal party supporters.

As for the more basic issue, it is argued that something like a Senate is required to act as a check on the first House to make sure that it does not pass hastily drawn or ill-conceived legislation. There have been occasions when the Senate has served this purpose, but they have been few and far between and have hardly involved issues of profound national concern. Moreover, reform of the House and particularly of its committees would greatly lessen the likelihood of hastily drawn and ill-conceived legislation being enacted.

Reform of the House's committees brings to mind the one major claim to usefulness that the Senate has been able to make for itself over the past few years. That claim relates to the work of some of its special committees which have at times done some useful investigatory work. Here again, however, proper use of revitalized House committees would obviate the need for any such Senate committee work. Thus, it is hard to imagine any role that the Senate now plays that could not be just as well discharged by our elected representatives.

This brings me to the present composition of the Senate. It is sad but true to say that, for the most part, it is a haven for political has-beens. Most senators owe their appointments to the fact that they were faithful servants, effective fundraisers, or loyal representatives for their parties. And this remains the case despite pledges by one prime minister after another that he would not make the traditional types of appointments. Although Trudeau made pledges to the contrary, he fell into the traditional pattern. Most of the senators he appointed were nothing more than time-worn functionaries of the federal and provincial wings of his party. As if to indicate how cynical the whole process had become, Trudeau appointed one or two opposition members who were too effective for his liking and one token labor leader who was not then, and is not now, part of the mainstream of the labor movement.

If one looks at the overall results of this whole process, it is hardly surprising that the Senate should resemble a corporate board of directors more than a legislative assembly. It is about as representative of the Canadian public as the board of Argus Corporation or Brascan. Its membership reads like a Who's Who of the business and corporate community. This is only natural given the importance the Liberals and Tories have attached to rewarding their corporate fundraisers by providing them with a Senate resting place to complement their remaining company directorships.

One might say, not altogether facetiously, that the only case to be made for retention of the Senate rests on the greater harm its members might do if granted other forms of patronage. After all, they could be granted a board directorship on a crown corporation or membership on one of our many regulatory tribunals. It is frightening to think of what some of their vested interests might lead them to do on those bodies. And yet, at least some of them might be able to apply their limited backgrounds more usefully in these kinds of settings than in the Senate.

To me, the case for abolishing the Senate is unassailable. It is largely an unnecessary appendage to our federal legislative process. But worse still, it verges on the corrupt and fraudulent because of the narrow characteristics and criteria which are employed in the selection of its members.

Reforming the Senate

There are so many proposals for reforming the Senate that one hardly knows where to start. This multiplicity of proposals reflects the fact that not even the most aged, decrepit, and senile senator would any longer dare defend the institution in its present form.

Just as there are two fundamental grounds for abolishing the Senate, there are two distinct sets of proposals for reforming it. The first set revolves around the intended role of the Senate as a protector of provincial and regional interests at the national level. I did not mention this purpose in the previous section because the original idea was blurred, if not completely thwarted, from the outset by the fact that federal government appointments have been based almost exclusively on party loyalty. Individuals selected on this basis have usually, and not unnaturally, proven more faithful to their national party interests than to those of their provinces or regions.

To overcome this problem, the Tories now propose to call the Senate the "House of the Provinces," which has left the Liberals stuck with the label "House of the Federation" in order to differentiate their product. Both parties want at least half of the members of the new second House to be appointed by the parties in the provinces, proportional either to their votes in the last federal or the last provincial election. Once one allows for the many other proposals which are floating around, the possible combinations and permutations multiply greatly.

However it is constituted, the notion of a House of the Provinces or Federation could prove very disruptive to the ongoing federal governance of this country. It would, in effect, further institutionalize federal-provincial conflict at the national level. Depending on how much power the new second House were granted, it could end up tying the national legislative process in knots. Surely we are developing enough other federal-provincial checks and balances without further institutionalizing the process within a second national legislative chamber.

Aside from the powers and purposes of such a chamber, there is the question of how its members should be selected. Appointment seems to remain the favored approach, if only to avoid a head-on confrontation between two elected bodies. If this is to be the case, the question is who should do the appointing. If we retain anything like the present Senate, the opposition parties should have the right to name their due proportion of members, based on the breakdown of votes in the last federal election. Perhaps every party should have to announce in advance of an election a special party list for this purpose. It becomes even more complicated if we move toward some degree of provincial involvement à la a House of the Provinces or Federation. Assuming we do that, I would argue that the federal parties should be able to appoint at least one-half of such a chamber, again based on published party lists and the results of the last election.

Still other proposals would allow the major interest groups in the country to nominate some of the members of the second chamber. Thus, in the name of a modified version of corporatism, labor, management, the professions, and other groups might be allocated one-third of the members, while the remaining two-thirds would be divided between federal and provincial appointees. The possibilities are obviously limitless.

Last but not least is the proposal to elect all or part of the new upper chamber on the basis of proportional representation by province or region. Aside from the complexities that would be involved, if only because of the role of our minority parties, there is a more fundamental objection to this type of proposal. Even if the new upper House were granted only limited delaying powers on certain issues, the very fact that it were elected would undoubtedly predispose it to do just that to prove its worth. Surely the American example of the problems which can arise between two nationally elected tribunals should be enough to dissuade us from moving in that direction.

Conclusion

The Senate as it now stands can no longer be tolerated. The choice is between abolition and reform. None of the possible reforms is particularly appealing. Furthermore, most of them are designed to serve purposes better met by other means. It is time, therefore, to abolish the Senate. Its abolition is long overdue.

CHAPTER EIGHT

The Monarchy, Referenda, and the Supreme Court

VIRTUALLY EVERYTHING SEEMS to be up for grabs in the current constitutional debate in this country: the status of the monarchy is subject to reassessment; the notion of resorting to a referendum on contentious public questions is being promoted; and various ideas have also been circulating concerning the role of the Supreme Court.

The Monarchy

One of the most encouraging agreements to emerge to date from the federal-provincial deliberations of our first ministers is that pertaining to the monarchy. Despite some federal proposals to the contrary, it now appears to have been agreed that the principle of the monarchy will remain unchanged. This means that the Queen and her agents the governor-general and the lieutenant governors will continue to represent the symbolic heads of states both of our country as a whole and of the individual provinces.

While the basic role of the monarchy is symbolic, it can go beyond that in the event of a parliamentary crisis

growing out of the failure of any one party to carry a
majority of Parliament. Even then, however, there are
well-established precedents to be followed which very
much limit the discretionary power of a monarch or his
representative. The same limitations prevail in the case of
a monarch's historic power to appoint judges and
senators, give assent to all bills, and so on. It would be
unthinkable for a monarch to go against the will of the
government and Parliament on any such matters.

While it would, no doubt, be useful to clarify many of
these matters in our constitution, it may be best to leave
well enough alone. This is because of the risk of moving
toward a more presidential or republican style of government in which there might be the temptation to
combine the office of prime minister and chief of state. It
was conceivable to read such a possibility into the Liberal
government's proposals on the monarchy. This was
enough in itself to warrant anxiety; one couldn't help
being relieved when the first ministers agreed to continue
to accept the monarchy's current status.

Referendum Pros and Cons

From time to time, the idea of a referendum on a major
policy issue resurfaces in Canada. By special acts of
Parliament, two such referenda have been held in
Canada — one on prohibition in 1898, the other on
conscription in 1942. In both cases, incidentally, the
government chose to ignore the results.

Two recent developments have tended to popularize
the idea of a referendum. One is Proposition 13 in
California which forced a drastic cut in local property
taxes. Ridiculously simplistic in form, this proposition

had so much appeal it was almost certain to pass. It has since captured public imagination all over North America and throughout the Western World as one possible means of curbing the unlimited revenue demands we place upon our governments by continually demanding more services of them.

Closer to home, a second development has been the Parti Québécois victory in Québec, together with its pledge to hold a referendum on separation. Prompted by concern over the vagueness of the wording which the PQ might employ in its referendum, the former Liberal government introduced legislation which would have permitted it to run a referendum of its own, nationally or provincially, either on the issue of separation or any other constitutional matter.

The strongest case for the referendum — or its close cousins the initiative and the recall — is that it represents a form of direct democracy. It lets the people decide a major issue on the basis of their own consciences, rather than on the politics of their elected representatives. In the absence of a free vote, the latter do not vote according to their consciences let alone according to those of their constituents. Instead, they vote on the basis of their party position, which is only one of many it has on any number of issues. This being the case, the voter cannot really back a party on any one question, but rather must select one on the basis of a composite of questions. Referenda and the like get around this dilemma by permitting citizens to vote on individual issues.

As appealing as the case for direct democracy in any form may be, there are good arguments to be raised against referenda. Some of these arguments are easy to get around, such as the possible undermining of minority rights by majorities. A strong bill of rights would preclude this possibility. More difficult to circumvent, however, would be the oversimplification of complex issues. If this happened, it would serve to polarize more than anything else. Issues such as abortion and capital punishment, for example, do not lend themselves to black or white answers. Then there is the even greater danger of the detraction from, or evasion of, government responsibility which is the very basis of parliamentary democracy. Proposition 13 in California, which places an arbitrary limit on real estate taxes across the state regardless of local concerns, provides an illustration of this sort of phenomenon.

For these reasons, referenda and the like should be confined to the most fundamental questions on which governments themselves have agreed that the public's views should be ascertained on a direct basis, if only for advisory purposes. Québec's separation from the rest of Canada is one such question, although rival federal and provincial referenda with or without loaded language may not serve to clarify but just to confuse matters.

The Supreme Court

Since the Supreme Court represents the final court of appeal in the land, proposals for its reform must be treated with great care. It is the ultimate interpreter of our bill of rights and constitution and of every federal and provincial statute in the country. Its fundamental significance cannot be overestimated. This is why it is imperative that its members be of the highest caliber. Nothing should be countenanced which detracts from that imperative.

Any body like the Supreme Court is bound to be a source of controversy from time to time. Such controversy is especially likely in the constitutional sphere when federal-provincial relations are in a state of flux. Those who favor decentralization are bound to be critical of a body seemingly supportive of a strong, central government. It hardly seems to matter that such criticism should be directed at the constitution or statute being interpreted rather than the body trying to apply it.

A number of recent decisions have made the court appear decidedly pro-federal. These decisions include those upholding the federal government's authority over wage and price controls and cable television. Equally contentious was another case in which the court held that the federal government's control over interprovincial or international trade took precedence over provincial management of natural resources.

If these Supreme Court decisions are indeed too pro-federal, the real fault does not lie so much with the court as with the BNA Act. The solution is not to meddle with the court's powers or the appointment of its members. Instead, it is to change the BNA Act. Yet, that is obviously not the focus of attention when it comes to current criticisms of the Supreme Court.

Proposals to reform the Supreme Court now abound. Even the former Liberal government was contemplating major surgery. It would have enlarged the court from nine to eleven members, increased Québec's share from three to four, and guaranteed each region at least one member. In addition, only the justices from Québec could have heard cases involving the civil law of that province, although they would have been free to hear all others as well. Worse still, all Supreme Court appointments would have

been subject to debate and ratification by a revised Senate
which was to be called the House of the Federation.

Like virtually all other proposals for reform of the
Supreme Court, these were clearly designed to deflect its
political and regional critics. In effect, they served to make
the court one of the leading scapegoats for our problems
of national unity and regional alienation. They ignored
and placed in jeopardy the need to attract the most
qualified jurists in the land to serve on the court. They
risked the crucial role of the court as the dispenser of law
and justice for the sake of misdirected political purposes.

If the court has been too centrist in its rulings, the task
is to amend the BNA Act. The only minor changes that I
would make in the court itself concern the procedures for
appointments. The federal government must more
formally consult both the provinces and the bar associations before making its selections. To go any further than
this, however, would be to politicize the body to the
jeopardy of its essential judicial character.

CHAPTER NINE

Bureaucrats, Regulators, and Royal Commissioners

CIVIL SERVANTS, MANDARINS, and regulators not only account for a large share of our tax dollars through their salaries, they also conjure up thoughts of all manner of government intrusions into our daily lives. Only royal commissioners do not seem to fit into this context. At least their impact is delayed or second-removed. Nonetheless, all of these various species both consume a high proportion of our resources and have at their disposal a tremendous potential for undue intervention in our affairs. More must be done to ensure that they do their jobs well and without unnecessary interference in the lives of the rest of us.

Contracting Out and the Public Sector in General

The government or public sector of this country now accounts for about forty percent of our GNP and around twenty percent of our labor force. Given its absolute and relative size, much more thought has to be given to its operation within our total system.

The basic problem with much of the government or public sector is that there is no bottom line. At least at the federal level, it cannot even go bankrupt. If the worst comes to the worst, the federal government can use the Bank of Canada to print more money to cover its losses. In effect, this is what it has been doing over the past few years.

When an enterprise cannot go out of business, it simply is not under enough pressure to produce. It does not have to be efficient, innovative, and productive to survive. Especially when it is in a near monopoly situation, it can charge any price it wants. About all that can stop it is a taxpayer rebellion and even that may not be sufficient if the service provided is of an essential nature.

The challenge is clearly to make the civil service more competitive. It is at this point that I would make a distinction between the provision of public services and the way they are provided. I have always felt that many public services were so vital that the government should see to their provision. But that is different from saying that they should be provided by government. What one should emphasize is the need for government to make sure such services are delivered. How they are actually delivered is another matter.

What I would stress is the case for contracting out more public services on the basis of competitive tenders. Union criticism of such a practice could be defused, though not eliminated, by specifying that all those bidding on such tenders must agree to a payroll package roughly equivalent to that in the public service. Then it would be largely a matter of who could do the job better.

In keeping with this approach, I would argue that a significant fraction of most public services should always be contracted out as a means of keeping the rest of the service in question on its toes. Where private enterprise demonstrates it can do the job better, that fraction should be increased. But it should never diminish to zero, if only because some part of every public service should always remain in the government sphere in order to provide a countercheck on what the private contractors are up to.

Nothing short of this kind of approach will do the job. Concepts like zero base budgeting may have some effect, but the best check on any service is competition.

Coping with the Mandarins

One of the most frightening things about our governments is the bureaucracy that envelops them. To a certain extent, this is just a reflection of size and therefore a characteristic of any large organization. Even allowing for this consideration, it is more menacing in the public service for two reasons. The lesser of the two relates to the lack of competition afflicting the public service — a problem already dealt with. In the absence of competition, bureaucracies can tie themselves in endless knots without any fear of the consequences.

Even more serious is the effect this can have on policy making at the highest levels of government. Bureaucracies develop such vested interests in their policies, priorities, and programs that their resistance to change is often immense. This is most likely to show up when a government changes hands after one party has been in power for a long time. That party's leaders will have appointed all the senior civil servants or mandarins who are bound to feel some loyalties toward those leaders and their policies, if not the party itself. It can then become most difficult for a new government to move both the senior civil servants or the mandarins and their bureaucracies in new directions.

The Americans get around this problem by having the entire senior management of the administration and civil service resign after every presidential election. This can have a very unsettling effect since thousands of jobs are involved. This is the opposite extreme of our own system under which deputy ministers, assistant deputy ministers, and their equivalents normally carry on from one government to another. We assume that the civil service is neutral from top to bottom and consequently can serve any government equally well.

I do not buy this proposition, at least not at the top levels in the civil service. Deputy ministers and assistant deputy ministers work too closely with their ministers not to form close relationships. New governments and their ministers should feel free to replace these key individuals. As in the States, they should be expected to resign upon a change of government.

Some will argue that few civil servants would become deputy ministers or assistant deputy ministers under such a system. This could be a problem, although it could be partially resolved by granting any displaced individuals who did not choose to leave the public service other, less responsible positions. Assuming it did remain a serious problem, though, I am not sure it would be devastating. In fact, it could have its advantages. One of the reasons the U.S. experiences so much interaction between government and other groups in society is precisely because so many positions become vacant when the presidency changes. Many of the incumbents move out into the private sector of the economy from which many of their replacements are also drawn. Canada would obviously benefit from some of this interchange which is now almost totally lacking from our system largely because of the entrenched positions enjoyed by our senior civil servants.

Regulation and Deregulation

As a people, we have surrounded ourselves with so many regulations and regulatory bodies that it is little wonder that deregulation has become a popular political rallying cry. Obviously there are many regulations that we cannot do without. These range from our traffic laws to standards for weights and measures. The difficulty, however, is to decide where to draw the line.

There are many problems and therefore many solutions required in the regulatory sphere. One growing problem is the cost of regulation. In business and commerce, the paper burden alone is enough to drown all but the largest enterprises, and they are spending a fortune to keep up with it. The notion of sunset laws or some other system which would ensure periodic review of the administrative and other costs involved in various types of regulation might be useful.

In the area of environmental and health and safety regulation, more emphasis must be placed on the costs as well as the benefits. Under U.S. federal law, every new regulation is now supposed to be subject to an economic impact assessment. This is intended to reduce the proliferation of regulations which do not take into account economic costs. We could certainly profit from a similar requirement in Canada where the net benefits of regulation are more or less taken for granted.

Regulations designed to serve the public interest may also be perverted to serve the private interests of those they are supposed to control. All manner of agricultural marketing boards and rate-setting agencies immediately spring to mind in this connection. Just how costly regulation can prove to be to the consumer has been demonstrated by the significant fall in airline fares in the U.S. since the protective cocoon of regulations was removed from that industry. Just how resistant industry can prove to be to the very thought of competition is equally well demonstrated by the resistance U.S. trucking labor and management are showing to the threat of deregulation in their industry.

There is no easy way to ensure that regulation is not misused by those it is intended to police. A couple of ideas come readily to mind. Perhaps those serving on regulatory bodies should also have to resign when a government changes hands. That would ensure a massive infusion of new blood every few years. Short of this, there should at least be something approaching the American federal requirement that a minority serving on such bodies be drawn from the ranks of the opposition party. In addition, some of the members on such bodies should be drawn from nominees suggested by public interest groups such as the Consumers' Association of Canada and Pollution Probe.

Deregulation should be promoted wherever the costs of regulation can be shown to have overrun the benefits. But the pledge of deregulation is not enough on its own to do the job. The need for a great deal of regulation will always remain in our complex, interdependent society. This means that more devices such as representation by public interest groups must be built into regulatory processes in order to ensure that they serve the purposes intended.

Royal Commissions and Task Forces

This country has a long tradition of using royal commissions, and more recently task forces, as a means of defusing controversial issues so as to delay any adverse political impact on the party in power. Occasionally, royal commissions are appointed solely for the more legitimate purpose of analysis and scrutiny of a troublesome social issue, but this has been the exception rather than the rule.

We can hope that most, if not all, royal commissions and task forces will become redundant and unnecessary if the committee structure of the Parliament of Canada is revitalized. Certainly, more active and well-supported parliamentary committees should obviate the need for many royal commissions and task forces. Governments will, no doubt, still want to name some — if only to try to place certain contentious matters outside Parliament's reach for a time.

To reduce this temptation, I would propose a new method for appointing royal commissioners and task force members. This proposal is made on the assumption that such bodies are intended to serve Parliament and the public, rather than the party in power. This being the case, they should be far more representative than they are. To this end, I would argue that no royal commissioners or task force members should be named by a government except by agreement with the leader of the opposition. Failing such agreement, the members should be named by the chief justice or his provincial counterpart.

This would put an end to loaded royal commissions or task forces such as the present federal McDonald and Québec Keable inquiries into wrongdoing by the RCMP. Both bodies were preselected by governments seeking certain findings which they were more likely to receive from past, if not present, supporters. In this instance, we could probably have anticipated a more balanced result if the two commissions had been combined.

No more inquiries of this kind should be launched without less partisan appointees to undertake them. Even this may not prove enough if governments choose to load their terms of reference. If that pattern should persist, then maybe the leader of the opposition should also have to agree on the royal commission's or task force's terms of reference, as well.

CHAPTER TEN

An Industrial Strategy for Canada

THE TERM "INDUSTRIAL strategy" is one we could well do without. Unfortunately, it is now so widely used that it has virtually preempted any other. What it implies is the search for a more viable industrial base or structure for this country. That is something we have been seeking since our inception. It requires as much attention now as it ever did, given the alternatives with which we must now come to terms.

Under the National Policy

Prior to the introduction of our national policy in 1878 and, indeed, for many years thereafter, Canada was a very primitive industrial society. Today, we would describe what we were then as "hewers of wood and drawers of water." Agriculture, forestry, and the fur trade were the mainstays of our economy. Manufacturing was highly localized and confined to the most simple of goods. Anything very large or complicated was imported from abroad.

Discontent and frustration with this primitive status

led us to promulgate our national policy. High tariff walls were erected in order to establish a protected domestic market for manufactured goods. In time, this did have the desired effect as more and more manufacturing was attracted to the country. Not all of it was Canadian managed or owned. Gradually, more and more foreign firms simply chose to jump over our tariff barriers by establishing subsidiaries to service the Canadian market.

Equally disconcerting was the violation of one of the basic tenets of our national policy. This tenet was that our industries would only require tariff protection while they were infants. Eventually, we postulated, they would grow up big and strong and able to survive on their own without any protection. In most cases this did not happen — in part, no doubt, because the same tariffs that encouraged industry to come in also sheltered it from competition. Our industries did not have to compete in order to survive.

Nurtured by the national policy, Canada did develop a wide base of infant industries by the late 1920s. After slowing down during the depression of the 1930s, most of these industries took off during World War II and its aftermath. Canada's obvious, but unnatural, advantages during those strife-torn years allowed us to develop delusions of grandeur concerning our industrial capacity and strength. Yet our manufacturing never became competitive enough to cope with its U.S. counterpart, let alone with the recovery of industry in Western Europe and elsewhere. Nor can much of it hope to compete with the burgeoning manufacturing industries in the developing countries.

As Canada moved into the 1950s and 1960s, its

economic strength reverted back to dependence on its traditional resource industries. The international advantage in terms of trade shifted in favor of these industries, and we had a resource boom the likes of which we had never seen before. In addition to our forest products and minerals, oil and gas became more and more important as an energy-short world was forced to pay a premium for these products.

For the most part, our manufacturing industries had to rest content with supplying the domestic market. They were at a twofold disadvantage in terms of competing for exports. They had neither the advantage of volume and economies of scale of our large Western trading partners nor the cheap labor costs of the developing countries. Increasingly, it became a matter of whether they could even compete with imports into the country. This will now be put to a more severe test as a result of the latest round of tariff reductions under the General Agreement on Trade and Tariffs (GATT) which has led to a general freeing-up of trade.

But the situation is not as bleak as it has been made to read. Our Canadian-owned steel industry has become one of the most efficient, innovative, and productive in the world. The same can be said of our banks which rank among the best-run institutions of their kind in the world. In many other high technology fields we have firms which are doing extremely well. Current examples are to be found in the fields of both fiberoptics and telecommunications. In the critical automotive industry we have entered into a generally advantageous pact with the U.S. which has created a North American common market for automobiles and their parts.

At the other extreme, however, we have untenable

situations which are going to be very difficult to resolve. We have a huge textile industry employing approximately 150,000 people in Québec alone which, by its own admission, could not survive competition from the developing countries without a tariff wall around it. While this is protecting the jobs of those employed in this industry, it is costing Canadian consumers a fortune. It is also making it difficult to make the kinds of trade concessions to others which we must if we want them in turn to open up their markets to our more competitive products.

The Search for an Alternative

There seems to be fairly widespread agreement in Canada today that the status quo will no longer suffice in terms of our present industrial structure. But that is about as far as the consensus goes. As for what we should do now, there is a great deal of argument. At one extreme, there are those who favor what I would describe as a kind of "Fortress Canada" approach. They would restore even higher tariff barriers than we now maintain in order to preserve as diversified a manufacturing base as possible. Aside from the fact that such a policy would violate GATT and invite retaliation, it would probably even prove unacceptable to Canadians once the adverse impact on our standard of living became apparent.

At the other end of the spectrum are those who would rely on those sectors of our economy which can continue to compete internationally without protection. They tend to advocate freer trade based on multilateral tariff reductions allowing in time for the chips to fall where they may. It does not bother them that this might mean the loss of many of our manufacturing industries. They believe this would be offset by a continuing resource boom and by our highly competitive banks and other service industries moving into the international sphere. To the accusation that this would return us to being essentially hewers of wood and drawers of water, they wonder whether that would be so bad if it yielded a high standard of living. Neither do they seem perturbed by the industrial dislocation which would occur nor by the heightened vulnerability to which we would be subject due to the vicissitudes of international politics and trade.

In between these two extremes are several other options involving varying degrees of restructuring and specialization within Canadian industry. Each one of these options involves a degree of government intervention to promote those Canadian industries most likely to survive the rigors of international trade. One variation on this approach would feature broad framework policies in such areas as competition, manpower, and research and development designed to assist the natural winners in the marketplace. This approach would leave it largely up to competitive forces to sort out who would and would not receive such assistance.

The other variation on this theme would have the government decide on our best bets industrially and assist them in every way possible. Presumably, any such decisions would be made in concert or, at least, after consultation with industry in general. This possibility, however, suggests impossible political dilemmas. After all, it would require governments to choose between our potential winners and losers — a choice which would hardly endear them to everyone. Worse than the political risks involved, of course, is the very real possibility that the government could be wrong in its choices.

This brings me to the alternative I am reluctantly inclined to favor: closer economic ties — perhaps eventually even total economic integration — with the U.S. This option provokes so many nationalist war cries and is accompanied by so many risks in terms of our political and social sovereignty that it merits a section — indeed a section and another chapter — to itself. In the meantime, it is worth expanding on some of the foregoing options since it is the difficulty of achieving any of them which continually drives me back to the American alternative.

The idea of a new national policy for Canada seems to be based on the notion that we can do many things that could prove impossible. First, there is the presumption that we can somehow select a few key industries where we really do have a long-run, comparative advantage. Recent suggestions have included the fiberoptics and telecommunications industries where we have been in the forefront of a number of technological advances. Having selected those industries, we would give them every form of special encouragement, especially with research and development. Of course, we might somehow have to "Canadianize" them (that is surely a more palatable term than nationalization) to make sure that they would apply the fruits of this research and development in this country. As we were doing all this, we would go along with multilateral tariff reductions on an across-the-board basis, thereby ensuring our newly favored industries access to markets large enough to enable them to realize economies of scale.

As these industries were expanding into newly opened world markets, our less favored and presumably less competitive or natural industries would be taking a beating from more fortunately placed foreign rivals. But that would be all right, provided there were transitional arrangements because the slack resulting from this process could be more than taken up by the expanding industries on which we had placed our reliance. In time, we would end up with a more viable long-run industrial structure.

I have several problems with this analysis, although I see one great advantage to it. At least, it recognizes that we cannot go on trying to produce the same full range of goods and services as the U.S. with only ten percent of its market size. To try to do so would really involve a kind of "Fortress Canada" mentality with isolation and self-sufficiency as our rallying cry. The results of such a narrow, nationalistic approach would be disastrous in terms of our standard of living alone, not to mention any other variables.

But let me return to the problems I envisage in attempting to concentrate on a more limited range of specialized industries capable of competing in the world at large. The basic problem is that I don't know how we are to get from here to there. There is no way we could leave it to the market since its results would be quite unpredictable in the short run, if not in the long run as well. There is no way we could be sure that the market would settle for the industries we favored. In fact, if left to its own workings, it might well lead quickly to the second extreme I mentioned above — the one involving major emphasis on our most competitive resource and service industries.

Since the results of the market could prove quite contrary to that supported by any new national policy, those behind it are not going to be prepared to trust the market. This means that the government or Parliament or some grand tripartite body might have to engineer the desired result. Assuming their willingness to try to do so, this means only one thing to me — Ottawa would take over the whole exercise. For reasons already alluded to earlier in this volume, I would place much more faith in the so-called invisible hand of the marketplace than in the visible hand of any government decision-maker.

It's not just that I don't trust the latter. Even if they didn't take over the exercise, there is the question of whether our newly chosen infant industries would be any more likely to grow up than those nurtured by our original national policy. Moreover, even if we chose the right industries, and they did grow up to be competitive on a world scale, we could not be sure how long they would have access to those markets. Whereas the "Fortress Canada" option would make us too inward-looking, this option could make us too outward-looking in a world apparently more dedicated to regional economic groupings than to a wide-open global market.

The American Option

This brings me back to the option I have come to favor— that is, closer economic relations with the U.S., despite all the risks involved. Canada is one of the few relatively industrialized countries in the world which does not have ready access to a market of at least 100 million people. We all know we need such access, yet we are afraid to turn to our neighbor to the south which provides by far the most logical market of this size for our goods and services.

For ten years now we have been trying to lessen our

dependence on the U.S. market. This was what Trudeau's third option was all about. We were going to increase our trade with Western Europe and the Far East, thereby enabling a reduction of our trade with the U.S. But it hasn't worked and it won't work. There are two oceans and many other obstacles standing in the way of this third option. Despite a decade of effort to exploit it, the percentage of our overall trade with the U.S. has increased steadily both in terms of exports and imports.

The U.S. has always been our most logical trading partner. Canada was founded and persists in defiance of that fact. We force a great deal of trade east and west within Canada, when by nature most of it should flow north and south. It is time we again confronted this reality and figured out how to take maximum advantage of it. Part of this challenge is economic. That part will be dealt with here. But part of it relates to the question of whether we can move in the U.S. direction economically without jeopardizing our political and social sovereignty. This is the more emotional side of the issue which I will leave to the next chapter.

If we are to move toward closer economic ties with the U.S., we have to consider the form these ties should take. In the extreme, we could work toward a common market with everything, including currency, eventually common. Short of that, we might settle for a free trade area, leaving us with our own currency and our own tariff structure against other foreign goods. Perhaps we would not even have to go as far as a common market or free trade area. It might be wiser to settle for a series of pacts such as the ones we have in the auto industry.

In advocating closer economic relations with the U.S., I would emphasize gradualism, phasing-in arrangements, and various adjustment and transitional measures. Because of this, I prefer the negotiation of a series of common markets in different industries. Presumably, this would involve some pairing. There are industries where integration would, no doubt, favor us more than the U.S. and vice versa. Only where there are roughly balanced, mutual advantages could we proceed on an industry-by-industry basis.

In the long run, I am prepared to risk economic union with the U.S. They might not settle for anything less and neither might we as we experienced the economic benefits of moving in that direction. Most of the Maritime and Prairie provinces would, no doubt, benefit immensely from such an arrangement. Only central Canada — the author and benefactor of our original national policy — would have any major economic concerns. And they could prove to be much more short term than long term. After all, central Canada is well placed to serve what is still a very lucrative part of the U.S. market.

Most of my misgivings and reservations about closer economic ties with the U.S. concern the noneconomic effects. I do, however, have one major economic concern. That relates to the more ready access Americans would have to our resources and especially to our oil and gas reserves. I am selfish enough to want to preserve them in so far as that is necessary to ensure an adequate Canadian supply. But I am also realistic enough to recognize that, with or without closer economic ties between our two countries, there is no way we will be able to withhold them from the U.S. if they become desperate for them.

CHAPTER ELEVEN

Canadian Nationalism and the U.S.A.

CANADIAN NATIONALISM HAS always been a difficult phenomenon to appraise. Except for its French-Canadian variation, a good deal of Canadian nationalism seems to take the form of anti-Americanism. This makes it all the more difficult to sort out the effects which closer economic ties with the U.S. might have in other areas. At stake, ultimately, would be our general autonomy, independence, and sovereignty.

English-Canadian Nationalism

Throughout most of Canada's history, English-Canadian nationalism has exhibited considerable pro-British and anti-American character. The role of the Empire Loyalists who fled the American Revolution is as good an early testimony to this characteristic as anything else. Although the Orange Order and the Imperial Order of the Daughters of the Empire do not have the influence they once had, they remain indicative of deeply held loyalties which extend far beyond their numbers. One only has to visit Victoria to realize that the British link is still alive and well in some parts of Canada. It could hardly be otherwise, given the number of our founding fathers and later emigrants who came from that country.

More complex is the English-Canadian love-hate relationship with the Americans. The liking or love we have for our neighbors to the south is reflected in our life styles. We are so similar in so many ways that anyone who is not from North America finds it difficult to comprehend why we claim to be different. We dress the same way, listen to the same music, and watch the same television. We work for many of the same companies and belong to many of the same unions. American culture permeates Canada's to the point where few can tell what is ours or theirs. One could go on *ad nauseum* bringing out close parallels.

And yet, underneath it all, there is a streak of anti-Americanism that runs deep in many of us. We pride ourselves on being different. We know we have less crime, we are sure we have better schools, and we are convinced we look after our disadvantaged and downtrodden better than they do. We don't have the civil rights problems they have, or a Vietnam on our conscience, or a Nixon and Watergate to try to forget. But saying that we don't want to be American is not quite the same as saying we want to be Canadian. The point is that so much of our nationalism has been more negative than positive.

The greatest exception to this ambivalence among English Canadians is to be found among those who have themselves emigrated from other countries. Most of these people have an appreciation of this country that few of the native born ever experience. They chose of their own volition to come here. They know what it is like to live elsewhere. They appreciate the difference or they would have gone back. Their feeling for Canada is so positive that they don't need any anti-Americanism to be nationalists.

It is hard to get a handle on the degree to which English-Canadian nationalism varies on a regional basis across the country. Sometimes one has the impression that Ontario represents the bastion of English-Canadian nationalism in the country. In contrast, if only because of their resentment of the traditional domination by the central provinces, it appears that the West in particular is less nationalistic. At times, for example, Edmonton and Alberta seem to have more in common with Houston and Texas than with the rest of Canada. Nonetheless, there still does appear to be a very high level of commitment to the preservation of an independent Canada across its English-Canadian regions.

English-Canadian nationalism may indeed run much deeper across Canada than many of us realize. It may just be that it is so low key that it is hard to detect except when it is tested. If this is the case, there is much to be said for it. Nationalism can take many dangerous and virulent forms which English Canadians may be fortunate to have been spared. Yet, in their own decent and quiet way, English Canadians could prove very nationalistic.

French-Canadian Nationalism

Nationalism is, in some ways, even more complicated in Québec because of its separatist aspirations. For a long time, many French Canadians have thought of themselves as Québecois first and Canadians second. This is in sharp contrast with the situation among the majority of people in the other provinces who clearly think of themselves first and foremost as Canadians.

French-Canadian nationalism is easier to pinpoint than English-Canadian nationalism if only because of its separate language and culture. This has provided it with something distinctive to cling to and made anti-Americanism a less important ingredient. Recently, in fact, French-Canadian nationalism has featured more anti-English Canadianism than anti-Americanism.

As indicated earlier, French-Canadian nationalism has become a very emotional force and could, for this basic reason alone, drive the province to separate from the rest of Canada. There are so many French-Canadian groups developing a vested interest in some kind of special status, sovereignty-association, or outright separation that they cannot settle for anything less than one of these. The noneconomic benefits of such a status are so attractive to them that they would be willing to live with some economic costs to achieve their goal.

As indicated earlier, the problem with French-Canadian nationalism is that it could become a very intolerant and inward-looking force. As I mentioned, one only has to read of proposed laws calling for government licensing of all bookstores in Québec to appreciate where their nationalism could lead.

Nonetheless, on a more optimistic note, one must look at the benefits of French-Canadian nationalism not only from the vantage point of the Québecois but also from an overall Canadian point of view. The French-Canadian component of Canada is what differentiates us the most from the U.S. and what protects us the most from the American melting-pot phenomenon. If only for this reason English Canadians should be as eager as French

Canadians to help French Canadians preserve their Québecois heritage. Assuming this requires special status for Québec — as I have already argued that it must — this is surely something we should all be willing to strive for as long as this status does not, in effect, amount to *de facto* separation.

The Risk of Absorption by the U.S.

Throughout our history, Canadians have been paranoid about the prospect of being absorbed by the U.S. We have always feared that America's so-called "manifest destiny" would lead it to take us over lock, stock, and barrel. This is why we get so upset at any new sign of increasing U.S. influence on anything from our culture to our economy. It is also the reason we have shied away from closer ties with the U.S. whenever that has become a distinct possibility.

Having advocated closer economic ties with the U.S., I cannot deny that this would have some adverse effects on our ability to maintain our independence in other areas. Indeed, the closer we come to economic union with the U.S., the more complete would be our economic dependence upon that country. Growing economic dependence would obviously lead to more political and social dependence. How far this process could go before a separate Canada became a fiction is difficult to say.

Those who hold that economic union would inevitably lead to total union cannot be dismissed lightly. Even in Western Europe, where no one country dominates and most countries involved pride themselves on their independence, the Common Market could well lead to other types of integration. In our case, we would be linking up economically with a giant at least ten times our size by any standard one chooses to draw upon, and we could well end up with little choice over where the process ended.

On the other side of the argument is the question of whether the U.S. would be interested in absorbing us totally. It might not even be interested in economic union. To go beyond that would have external international and internal political implications it might not even care to contemplate. Joining us in an economic union, while resisting any temptation it might have to absorb us further, would be a feather in its cap in terms of its reputation as a neocolonial power. Moreover, domestically the ramifications of taking in several new states might so threaten the present balance of political forces within the U.S. as to rule it out altogether.

This is to say nothing of what I hope and trust would be a desire among Canadians to preserve their sovereignty in noneconomic areas. Economic union could obviously compromise our autonomy in any number of direct and indirect ways. But it need not lead us to give up those political and social characteristics that are distinctively Canadian. The problem is that there may already be so few of these left that some would give them up without even trying to preserve them. That prospect aside, I see no reason for believing that economic union would necessarily lead to total absorption by the U.S. The risks would be greater but not so extreme as to prevail over a determined effort by Canadians to retain significant degrees of autonomy, independence, and sovereignty, in spheres other than strictly economic ones.

CHAPTER TWELVE

Coping with Inflation

THE THREAT OF continuing inflation poses the number one economic problem in this country. This is not because inflation is more costly than high unemployment or low growth. Rather, it is because we cannot come to grips with these and other serious economic problems unless we learn to cope with inflation.

There is no one answer to the problem of inflation. It has too many causes to lend itself to any easy or ready solutions. I have chosen to concentrate on some new institutions which I have long felt were necessary as part of any effort to tackle inflation simply because so few others pay enough attention to this side of the problem.

Some Basic Issues

It is best to start with the need for a realistic target rate of inflation. What that should be would have to be determined in relation to the rates of inflation of our major trading partners and especially that of the U.S. Even with a flexible foreign exchange rate, I would argue that a realistic target rate of inflation for us to pursue would be one only marginally below that of the U.S. As a major trading country, we are just too dependent on others to aim for a rate much below that.

As for the causes of inflation, I will be concentrating on those which I earlier labeled behavioral, institutional, and structural. In doing so, I do not mean to minimize the significance of our fiscal and monetary policies which must be more reponsible if we are to make any headway with inflation. When controls were imposed on this country in 1975, the federal government was beginning its series of massive annual deficts, some of the provinces were trying their best to do likewise, and the Bank of Canada was increasing the money supply at about twenty percent a year, if only to accommodate all this debt. These were far more fundamental causes of the surge of inflation then being experienced by the country than any excessive wage, fee, and profit increases, even if there were quite a few of these working their way through the system.

Although the Bank of Canada has charted a more restrained and sensible course since then, it has had to do so despite the continuance of massive government debts, particularly at the federal level. Unless governments can be persuaded to put their fiscal houses in order, the problem of inflation will persist. Yet, this is not to say that wise fiscal policy alone, let alone a wise combination of fiscal and monetary policies, could rid us of inflation. They are necessary, but not sufficient, prerequisites to a lower rate of inflation.

The Need for a Federal-Provincial Incomes and Costs Review Board

At this point in Canada it is hard to make the case for any kind of anti-inflation body. This is because we have witnessed a parade of five such bodies in the last ten years, and all were futile. Every conceivable form of political deception and hucksterism has been involved in this charade. Just to list the names of the various bodies is enough to disillusion one. It all began with the Prices and Incomes Commission in 1969. Then came the Food Prices Review Board. This was followed by the biggest albatross of all, the Anti-Inflation Board. Since its demise we have had the Centre for the Study of Inflation and Productivity and the National Commission on Inflation. One could not have done a better job of discrediting any kind of anti-inflation tribunal if one had deliberately set about to do so.

In all of these institutional attempts to wrestle inflation to the ground, the most we have tried are guidelines or controls to deal with excessive claims made by all manner of groups against the rest of the system. The Anti-Inflation Board and its controls were designed to roll back excessive wages, fees, and profits. In doing so, they caused all manner of anomalies, distortions, and inequities. As elsewhere, they also set the stage for something between the income bubble and explosion we are now experiencing.

The worst thing about controls is that they deal with the symptoms of our inflationary problems rather than the problems themselves. If there are excessive wages, fees, and profits being imposed on the system, what you have to get at is the power behind the groups which are able to extract such concessions. Otherwise, you haven't really dealt with the source of the problem.

To begin to cope with the real problem, which is power and its abuse by all manner of groups, we require a new monitoring body with a sweeping mandate to identify such situations and to recommend appropriate remedial action. I believe it is so critical to have such a body I would provide it with the status of the auditor general and allow it to be dissolved only by joint address of the Parliament of Canada and some weighted combination of the provincial legislatures. This agency would need a federal-provincial character because the problems it would expose would be bound to fall within both jurisdictions.

As for the composition of such an agency, it should represent both levels of government, plus the major economic interest groups in the country. One possible composition would be one federal and two provincial nominees as well as one each from labor, management, the professions, agriculture, and consumers. These nominees should sever all their previous institutional links and enjoy a status similar to that of judges. While a group this diverse might occasionally have difficulty coming to an agreement, on most issues it would be one or two against the rest. This might lead to some mutual back-scratching, but I would be prepared to take that risk.

The primary responsibility of this monitoring agency should be to keep track of every major income and cost movement in the country. Whenever a wage rate, fee, profit, or what have you moves up significantly faster than the general index for its category, it should be subject to cursory examination. Where such examination reveals a prima facie reason for suspicion, it should be subject to more thorough study. If such a study bears out the suspicion, public hearings should be held to compel the offending group to explain what it has been up to.

Sometimes, the explanation will be an economic or market one, reflecting demand overrunning supply. Where that is the case, it would be extremely useful to have the monitoring agency lend its name to the explanation. Then, the public might better appreciate why a particular group was being permitted to extract more than its share of the current increases in incomes.

Where there is no economic or market justification for an above-average rise in an income or cost, it would be up to the monitoring agency to expose the real cause and to suggest an appropriate remedy. As the next chapter will reveal, most groups in our society enjoy special prerogatives and privileges granted to them by government legislation or regulation. No such privileges are sacrosanct, however, and they should be reviewed periodically. It makes even more sense to reassess their validity when the demands a group is making upon the economy are demonstrably out of line.

The basic premise of this whole approach is that no group behaves in the public interest unless it is in its own self-interest to do so. Right now, the fact of the matter is that it is in no one's self-interest to behave in the public interest. Any number of groups are running roughshod over the rest of us, and none of them are being called to account for doing so. Under these circumstances, it is foolish for anyone to behave responsibly lest they are left behind by the rest.

Two threats are necessary before groups can be expected to behave in the public interest in their own self-interest. One is disclosure and exposure of what they have been up to. Every group has skeletons in its closets which it does not want revealed, let alone subjected to public scrutiny. The other, and more important, threat is loss of power. Whether it is a hiring hall in a union, self-licensing in a profession, or a regulation, subsidy or tariff affecting a corporation, all groups have something to lose. They all must be made to feel that if they get out of line, they may be the next to be exposed for what they have been doing and the next to be cut down to size.

Of all the flaws to which this whole approach may be subject, perhaps the most fundamental concerns the follow-up role of politicians. If we had an effective monitoring agency and it was doing its job well, it is debatable whether politicians would follow up on its advice and counsel. After all, they would, in effect, be compelled to crack down on power and its abuse even among those groups backing their particular parties. I would not hold out much promise for this under present circumstances. But it might just prove possible if we could attract a new type of person into politics.

A National Economic and Social Council

The power of economic interest groups must not only be curbed when it is abused; it should also be channeled constructively whenever that is feasible. To this end, we require a national economic and social council comprised primarily of labor, management, and government representatives but including other interest groups as well. This body should be available to facilitate interaction between these groups on a consultative basis. No such body could go beyond an advisory role without running the risk of infringing upon Parliament's sovereignty.

The significance of an effective national economic and social council should not be minimized. In return for a greater input into economic and social policy formulation at the highest levels in this country, many, if not most, interest groups might be persuaded to moderate and temper the demands they place upon the overall system. If nothing else, they would at least have a better appreciation of the damage such demands could inflict upon the system.

Initially it would be foolhardy to expect very much from such a body. Experience has already indicated how difficult it is even to try to establish one. If, and when, one does get off the ground, all one could hope for is some consensus on the basic economic and social facts of life confronting this country. This, in itself, would be a great contribution since we now lack agreement on even the most elementary economic and social data. We do not even seem able to agree, for example, on such a straightforward issue as the overall wage differential between this country and the U.S.

In time, a national economic and social council might be able to move beyond the identification of the basic economic and social data confronting this country. Some day it might even play a part in helping us move toward a level and a distribution of income increases more consistent with our productivity and with the need to find a better balance between equity and incentive. But that is a complex and controversial subject which no group is about to face up to in this country.

A Council of Economic Advisors

To facilitate decision-making by both the federal and

provincial governments as well as the work of such bodies as the national economic and social council, we also require a variation on the U.S. Council of Economic Advisors. The main problem with the American council is that it is very much the handmaiden of the U.S. administration and cannot, therefore, be counted on for anything approaching nonpartisan, let alone objective, analysis. A better model would be West Germany's Committee of Five Wise Men which is composed of a more neutral cross-section of economists. Perhaps the solution in Canada would be to have the council appointed in a manner similar to that suggested for royal commissions — that is, by joint agreement of the prime minister and the leader of the opposition or, failing that, by the chief justice.

However appointed, a council of economic advisors should have a mandate to monitor the bahavior and performance of the Canadian economy on an annual basis or more often, when that is deemed necessary. The purpose of this mandate should be to provide as much information and insight as possible into the broad choices which seem to lie ahead. It is to be hoped this would provide an intelligent basis on which to initiate discussions in a national economic and social council and to make the difficult political decisions which governments must inevitably make.

A Standing Committee of Parliament on the Economy

To provide an effective focal point for an annual national debate on the state of the economy, there should be a standing committee of Parliament on the economy. This should be Parliament's single most important committee and is essential to its renewed role which I described in Chapter Six.

All of the new institutions recommended in this chapter should make their annual reports to this committee. This should not be a perfunctory exercise. These reports should be fully debated within the committee; afterwards, it should report its findings on each of them.

All the leading interest groups in the country should also be invited to present briefs to this committee. Again, there should be ample time provided for discussion in each case but with no obligation on the part of the committee to react formally to each of the briefs.

Finally, both the governor of the Bank of Canada and the minister of finance should present their annual reports before this committee. This procedure should cause no real difficulty as long as some of the unnecessary secrecy surrounding the preparation of the budget is terminated. As indicated earlier, such a step is long overdue.

Conclusion

Whether the central socio-economic problem of the day is inflation or something else, this country is desperately in need of a series of new institutions to help provide us with better control over our economic and social destiny. Several such institutions have been suggested in this chapter. The fact that the ultimate focal point of all this effort is an annual debate before the leading committee of Parliament is critical. It coincidentally emphasizes both the importance of the issues involved and of Parliament in their resolution.

CHAPTER THIRTEEN

Taming the Private Power Blocs

THE PREVIOUS CHAPTER emphasized the need to establish more checks and balances within our economic system. Only such checks and balances or the threat of them will induce the private power blocs in our society to behave more responsibly. Such checks and balances may be introduced through greater reliance on market forces. Failing that, it will require revised institutional arrangements based on the principle of countervailing power. It is now time to enlarge on these approaches as they might be applied to different interest groups.

The Labor Movement

It is my view that in the aggregate the labor movement in Canada is not too strong, but too weak. Experience in Western Europe in particular reveals that the labor movements which behave the most responsibly in terms of the public interest are the most powerful ones. Power may, as they say, be corrupting, but it can also be very sobering. The authority which has been acquired by the powerful Swedish and West German labor movements has almost compelled them to assume more responsibility for their behavior. No such statesmanlike role can be assumed by the Canadian labor movement because it is too weak even to entertain such an idea.

Having made the point that in the aggregate the Canadian labor movement is anything but too strong, let me hasten to add that this does not necessarily apply to all the individual unions involved. Indeed, there is no doubt that from time to time various unions enjoy too much power over employers and society at large. Just before controls were introduced in this country, this imbalance clearly applied in the case of some construction unions and some public service unions.

A selective, rather than an across-the-board, approach is required to deal with such imbalances. One such approach is now embodied in the concept of accreditation which allows a group of employers to band together collectively to form an employers' association. Such associations are granted the same exclusive bargaining rights afforded unions under our certification procedures. Through their associations, employers are able to confront unions on a more equal basis than they could on their own. The concept of accreditation has been applied most extensively in the construction industry, but it merits much wider application in industries where union divide-and-conquer tactics lead to leapfrogging. Prominent, current examples include the brewery industry, local municipalities, and supermarkets.

As for the public service, the most glaring illustration of a situation stacked in favor of unions exists at the federal level. Under the present system, unions benefit from a version of Russian roulette — played with the gun pointed toward the government, Parliament, and the public. Under the current federal system, unions alone are offered the choice of the conciliation-strike route or arbitration when there is an impasse in their negotiations with the government. This means that strong unions such as the air controllers and the postal workers usually opt for strike action, while weak unions invariably choose arbitration, because they know full well that this will secure them as much as the other unions win through strikes or the threat of strikes. Even when unions opt for the right to strike, the government has denied itself the right to lock out, one of the usual *quid pro quos* for the right to strike. This totally imbalanced system must obviously be overhauled if more sensible results are to emerge from the collective bargaining process in the federal public service.

In both the private and public collective bargaining arenas, many problems arise from the undue decentralization and fragmentation of our negotiating system. One only has to cite the situation in the airline industry to illustrate how serious this problem can become. Air Canada can be shut down by several different unions at different times, while several other unions can shut down the airports at still other times. This ludicrous situation must be corrected by ordering joint bargaining and common termination dates within these two separate sets of negotiating units, if not between them all as well. This would at least reduce the potential number of strikes from about a dozen to two. Yet only the British Columbia Labour Relations Board has been granted and has used the power to straighten out such chaotic situations.

Many other examples could be cited to illustrate the kinds of measures which have to be deployed to restore some balance to collective bargaining situations where power has become too lopsided in favor of organized labor. Many problems also result from power imbalances favoring management, but these are not the kinds of imbalances which the purpose of this chapter leads me to review. Suffice it to say that I am aware of numerous instances where our industrial relations system requires change in order to allow for these imbalances as well.

The Professions

Many professional groups enjoy unrestrained self-licensing, self-regulating, and fee-setting powers with which they can take advantage of the public. Such bodies insist on calling themselves associations, colleges, and societies — anything but unions — even though many of their activities are designed to serve precisely the same purposes as collective bargaining does for unions and workers.

There are many steps which could be taken when any professional group is found to be extracting excessive income increases in relation to other groups. The first step is to determine whether they should still enjoy self-licensing and self-regulating powers, let alone fee-setting ones. Assuming there is a strong public-interest case to be made for the continuation of any such powers, the question of public participation in their exercise should be carefully considered. Sometimes this purpose is supposedly served by public representatives sitting on professional licensing bodies and the like, but usually they are so token in number they are meaningless.

I believe at least one-third of the members of such bodies should be public members who might or might not be granted a vote. They should be nominated from a variety of sources, including consumer organizations, the labor movement, and management groups, as well as government. These public members should monitor the affairs of these professional bodies with a view to submitting an annual report to society at large on their view of the public stewardship of the profession in question.

As in the case of the labor movement, many other reforms could, no doubt, be imposed on professional groups proven to have abused their public trust. Permitting advertising by individual professionals is one such possibility which it is now restricted. My purpose has again been merely to bring out the fact that abuse by professional groups can be dealt with just as effectively as those by other groups.

The Business and Corporate Sphere

I must be even more cursory in my remarks about the business and corporate sphere than in the case of either the labor movement or the professions. It would be easy to write a whole book just about the challenge of keeping the business and corporate world competitive, let alone within the letter and spirit of the law. Members of the business and professional world profess to believe in the free-enterprise system, but they do not always practice what they preach. Where not engaged in collusive agreements to restrain trade, they are often shielded from competition through some government regulation, subsidy, or tariff. It is almost as if they believe in free enterprise for everybody but themselves.

For ten years now, this country has been struggling to enact a new competition policy. Such a policy is desperately needed to ensure that no anticompetitive actions are allowed to persist except where they can be shown to be operating in the public interest by facilitating necessary economies of scale or the like. Even then, there must be offsetting controls, such as lower tariffs, to make sure that the resulting benefits are passed on to the consumer.

As indicated earlier, it is also vitally important that we continually reassess all government regulations, subsidies, and tariffs designed to assist industry. So often what is initially implemented purportedly in the public interest ends up being manipulated almost exclusively in the private interest. Almost constant vigilance or at least regular periodic review must be introduced in the case of all such measures to ensure they are not abused.

Equally important is some sort of freedom of information law applying to corporations. As in the case of governments, they are permitted to hide too much from public view. This privilege is particularly worrisome in the case of multinational corporations which do not have to reveal their intercountry transfer payments. Such payments can be used for any number of suspect purposes including evasion of taxes. Canada should be in the forefront of countries calling for the publication of such data together with an explanation of it.

As in the case of professional groups, I would also recommend the naming of public members to some of our leading corporate boards or at least to those found guilty of transgressing the law. Again, such members should be named from a variety of sources and would have full voice but no vote. In order to prevent them from engaging in general fishing expeditions in the name of country, God, and parenthood, I would limit their mandate. Their task should be to submit an annual report to the body politic on their view of the public stewardship of the corporation in question in light of existing laws of the land, its advertising claims, its guarantees and warranties, and any codes of ethics to which it may have become party.

Farmers and Their Marketing Boards

What unions are to workers and professional groups are to their members, many marketing boards are or are becoming to farmers. Again, of course, what is done under the guise of marketing boards is purportedly being done in the public interest. We are told that by regularizing the flow of production in different agricultural commodities we will avoid the normal ups and downs occasioned by the imperfections of the marketplace. This will supposedly bring production and price benefits to both consumers and producers.

All of this sounds convincing until one perceives what the quotas and other regulations imposed on producers can do to the more efficient among them. Often they are compelled to operate at other than their optimum levels, with all the added costs attendant on such an approach. Perhaps this is all desirable if only to protect the family farm or for some other laudable social cause, but one is often left wondering about both the cause and its cost. At the very least, we once again require greater public participation in these marketing boards if they are not to be exploited primarily in the interests of those operating under them.

The Risk of a "Special Interest State"

I must add a major caveat to this chapter. It concerns the potential ability of the economic interest groups I have been examining to withstand any assault on their powers, prerogatives, and privileges. My misgivings and reservations on this score prevail despite, or perhaps because of, the fact that most if not all of these powers, prerogatives, or privileges were granted to these groups by government. At stake now is the latter's capacity and willingness to provide an effective system of checks and balances within the economy.

Throughout the Western world we are witnessing the emergence of what may be termed the "special interest state." By this is meant a state in which powerful private interest groups virtually compel the government to do their bidding or at least leave them alone. Through their determined lobbying such groups have already made the U.S. very vulnerable to such a menacing situation. Under these circumstances, the most the state can hope to do is to is to play the various groups off against each other.

This threat to democratic government makes it all the more imperative that we tackle major, out-of-line private economic interest groups before they do indeed become so powerful both economically and politically that no government can move against them. No doubt, some will argue that we have already passed that point. I refuse to accept this argument, but acknowledge that it is becoming more and more difficult to do so. I will have more to say on this frightening prospect in the final chapter.

CHAPTER FOURTEEN

A Social Priority for Canada

TWO INTERRELATED SOCIAL priorities currently attract my attention in this country. One concerns our tax system and leads me to recommend that we place much more emphasis on a comprehensive and progressive income tax. The other relates to our unbelievable mix of social security and public welfare programs which should be replaced by one or two guaranteed minimum income levels based on a negative income tax. In both of these highly sensitive areas of social policy, the challenge is to find an appropriate balance between equity and incentive considerations.

The Case for a Comprehensive and Progressive Income Tax

I have long favored a comprehensive and progressive income tax as the mainstay of our tax system. As for the comprehensiveness of the income tax, I believe very strongly that a dollar is a dollar no matter what its source. Thus, regardless of how income is derived — from work, capital gains, dividends, interest, gifts, inheritance or whatever — it should be treated as income for income tax purposes. The distinctions now drawn between some of these forms of income are inappropriate.

Take the distinction between income derived from work — primarily wages and salaries — and that derived from capital gains — much of which arises from little more than paper shuffling on Bay Street and its equivalents. It is hard for me to understand how we can countenance taxing income derived from work at a higher rate than that derived from capital gains. I might be able to accept this dichotomy if all or most capital gains resulted from direct and personal investment in new enterprises, products, and technology. But so much of it does not.

As for gifts and inheritance, I think they too should be included in one's taxable income, although I would in the case of inheritance consider spreading the impact of what would amount to estate taxes over a five to ten year period. Presently, most jurisdictions in Canada are moving in the opposite direction, toward freeing both gifts and inheritance from all forms of taxation. As indicated earlier, this is moving us increasingly away from a society based on equality of opportunity and toward one based largely on the accident of birth and class.

Turning to the matter of progressivity in our income tax system, I accept the argument that unduly high rates at the top do detract from incentive. I would be prepared to contemplate a maximum rate of fifty percent — but only on two conditions. The first relates to the comprehensiveness of the definition of income which I have just dealt with. The second grows out of the present mixture of our tax system which has been relying increasingly over the past few years on other forms of taxation. Corporation and sales taxes bother me the most as they are invariably passed on to the consumer and are thus regressive in nature. Corporation taxes also detract from the competitive position of our companies. I would want some assurance of a gradual shift away from these types of taxes and toward income taxes before I would lower the highest rates on the latter. Indeed, I would link these two moves.

In all of what I am proposing about our income taxes, I am motivated by the desire to make ability to pay the major criterion for determining our tax rates and structure. Only when this has an obvious deleterious effect on incentives would I back away from this priority. This is one of the reasons why we indexed the income tax system; we wanted to ensure that we were not taxed at a higher rate on unreal income increases based on inflationary gains. Yet we may have to back away from this otherwise sensible proposition if we cannot reduce government outflows accordingly so as not to drive the government into continuing massive deficits.

A Guaranteed Minimum Income

One of the ways we can begin to bring government expenditures under control is by reexamining our priorities in the social security and social welfare fields. Especially at the federal level, there is no use talking about any substantial cutbacks in spending unless expenditures in these areas are part of the process. There are several problems involved. The first relates to the massive bureaucracies which have been built up to service these areas.

An unbelievable proliferation of programs now exists to aid the disadvantaged and downtrodden in our society. There is unemployment insurance, workmen's compensation, old age assistance, and family allowances, to name only a few. Insofar as a minimum level of income maintenance is involved in such programs, we provide varying amounts depending on how the need for such assistance arose. The result is a "crazy quilt" pattern of social security and social welfare programs that defy description, let alone rationalization.

Even more disturbing to me is the fact that we have become so enamored of the principle of universality that need has little or nothing to do with many of the benefits involved. I have long queried why my mother is the beneficiary of a government pension, why my wife could collect unemployment insurance if she became unemployed, and why my children should be receiving family allowances. We cannot hope to balance the government's books, let alone do well by those really in need, as long as we insist on making payments to those in family units requiring no financial assistance.

My own preference is to see us gradually move toward a guaranteed minimum based on a negative income tax. If nothing else, such a move would allow us to dismantle some of the agencies which now exist to service our different income maintenance programs. The main argument against a guaranteed minimum income has to do with incentive, and I have some sympathy for it. With this in mind, I would be prepared to contemplate two minimum levels. The higher one would be for those permanently removed from the labor force through no fault of their own. This would include those occupationally incapacitated, those retired, and perhaps even single parents with special child-rearing problems. The other rate would cover those temporarily out of work and would be somewhat lower in order to leave them with the incentive to return to work as soon as possible.

I realize that the concept of a guaranteed minimum income presents many more problems than the ones I have dealt with. Nonetheless, I would urge that we move in this direction. It is the only way to tackle the income maintenance problem on a sound universal basis while trying to reconcile both the equity and the incentive considerations involved.

CHAPTER FIFTEEN

The Canadian Prospect

THE BASIC THRUST of this volume was intended to be the idea that this country and its people have everything going for them. While I believe this to be the case, I have spent so much time dwelling on our problems that the reader may have lost sight of my underlying theme.

It is now time to highlight the policy priorities which this country needs to meet the challenges facing it. I have neither ranked nor weighted these proposals; instead I would prefer to stress their interdependence. They obviously do not represent a package which must be bought in its totality, but they are a closely linked and consistent group of ideas.

Preserving Our Basic Freedoms

Whether in the form of freedom of speech or assembly or whatever, certain civil liberties are so essential that they should be enshrined in a bill of rights in a new constitution. Although our judiciary might not prove as vigilant in defense of these liberties as I would wish, this is still the surest way to protect these rights from everyone and everything, including politicians.

On the special question of bilingualism and biculturalism, I do not share the conventional wisdom in this country. Instead of bilingualism we should be talking about colingualism, with Québec basically French and the rest of the country essentially English. As for biculturalism, I hope and trust that it can be said to have given way to multiculturalism.

Another matter of great concern relates to the reconciliation of private rights and public security. National security is paramount to the survival of our nation, just as local police protection is vital to our daily life in peace and tranquility. But none of these prerequisites should be met at the undue sacrifice of civil liberties. All-party supervision of our national security forces and public review boards for our police forces could do much to resolve our problems in these areas.

Of equal importance to me is the issue of freedom of information in government. If only because information represents power, no government should be allowed to withhold anything from its citizenry for more than a limited period, unless it can prove that its release would unduly jeopardize the security of the country.

Improving Our Democratic Political Processes

If we are to improve our democratic political processes, nothing is more important than attracting more capable individuals to public life. The politician's job is a thankless one and we must offer higher salaries, more adequate expenses, and leaves of absence if we are to attract better candidates. In addition, we should consider a party-list system for the election of the leading members of each party. This would permit them to concentrate on the broader national issues by sparing them the petty and time-consuming rituals involved in local constituency politicking.

Assuming we do manage to attract more highly qualified individuals into a political career, we are going to have to make their work more meaningful and satisfying to retain them in that capacity. Among other things, this will require a major restructuring of Parliament designed to ensure that its committees play a more vital role in both the investigatory and legislative processes.

I am wary of a number of other proposed reforms in the political or quasi-political arena. I would prefer to abolish the Senate rather than try to reform it. I would not even try to replace it with a House of the Provinces or a House of the Federation. In the case of the monarchy I would be inclined to favor its present status rather than run the risk of turning our prime minister into a president. I am also dubious about resorting to referenda, although I do see such mechanisms having a place when it comes to such a critical issue as the severance of part of the country. I am even more dubious about purported reforms of the Supreme Court, especially when I find that the motivation is something other than securing the most competent jurists in the land to serve on this critical tribunal.

When it comes to the civil service bureaucracy, I am open to any number of suggestions to weaken its stranglehold on administration and policy formulation in the public arena. Among other things, I would attempt to contract out at least a fraction of every part of the public service if only as a check on the efficiency of the rest of it. Even more important to me is the possibility of a new government replacing all the deputy ministers and assistant deputy ministers in order to ensure sympathetic implementation of the changes it favors.

As for regulatory agencies, royal commissions, and the like, I would hope that a revitalized Parliament might eliminate the need for many of them. Those that were still necessary might be cured of many of their ills by ensuring a variety of sources of appointment so that no political party can load them with their hand-maidens.

Making Our Economic System Work

Two features were stressed in terms of the functioning of our economic system. One was dealt with under the guise of coping with inflation and primarily concerned the need to establish more effective checks and balances within our system. The second related to the purported need for an industrial strategy in this country and led to an exploration of the case to be made for closer economic ties with the U.S.

As for the first theme, I would argue that our competitive enterprise or market system, together with its complementary collective bargaining process, has served us well in the past and could continue to do so. But this is only likely to occur if certain remedial steps are taken. Among the most important of these is the need to crack down on abuse of economic power whether it occurs in labor, management, the professions, agriculture, or anywhere else including government itself. To alert us to such abuses of power and to fashion remedies to cope with them, we require a federal-provincial incomes and costs review board.

On the more positive side there is the need for a variety of new institutions in this country. We need some sort of national economic and social council involving these same groups to see if we can arrive at some common ground, if only on the nature of our problems and prospects. This arrangement, in turn, suggests the need for a reasonably independent and objective council of economic advisors to provide the basis for such deliberations. The results of this process should be placed before a standing committee of Parliament on the economy which should also hear from the minister of finance and the governor of the Bank of Canada as well as the major private interest groups.

As for the question of an industrial strategy, the critical challenge is to gain access to a wider market enabling us to benefit from the economies of scale that our competitors enjoy.

In my view, the most logical and natural answer for Canada involves closer economic ties with the U.S. Relatively speaking, I believe the benefits would be the greatest and the costs the least if we gradually moved in this direction.

Clarifying Our Social Priorities

Our social priorities should involve a commitment to a more equitable distribution of income as long as this does not have a serious adverse effect on incentives. To this end, I would move toward a greater reliance on our income tax system, both for government-revenue and social-transfer-payment purposes.

On the taxation side, I favor a comprehensive and progressive income tax but with a kind of tradeoff between these two priorities. As we make the income tax system more comprehensive in the sense of including virtually every form of income, I would lower the maximum rates levied. I believe the result would be a fairer tax system with no more adverse effects on incentive than the present one.

As for social transfer payments, I would like to see us move toward a guaranteed minimum income based on a negative income tax. If nothing else, this would surely help reduce the multiplicity of agencies which now exist to serve the needs of various types of assisted groups in our society. It might require a two-level floor, however, to distinguish between those in permanent need of assistance and those in only temporary difficulty who should be left with a strong incentive to return to work.

Retaining Our Sovereignty

The most critical challenge in terms of the maintenance of our sovereignty is to put our own house in order. This requires a resolution of our federal-provincial problems which entails several prerequisites that need only be underscored once again at this point. The first of these prerequisites amounts to a special status for Québec. Nothing less will do even if we have to find another name for the same thing. However, neither special status for Québec nor any other consideration should lead us to divide further what is already an unnecessarily balkanized national market in this country. It will be equally important to maintain a commitment to equalization payments in order to narrow the most extreme of the disparities which exist between our provinces and regions. Assuming we do move toward a more decentralized Confederation — as now seems almost inevitable— it will be essential to develop more effective federal-provincial and interprovincial coordinating mechanisms than are now in place.

The only significant external threat to our sovereignty results from the possibility of absorption by the U.S. This risk would obviously be heightened by the closer economic ties I have called for. Yet I would argue that economic union with the U.S. need not lead to political union with that country. That is only likely to occur if we fail to put our own house in order. This is the sense in which the greatest threat to our sovereignty is not external but internal. A reinvigorated Canadian Confederation need neither fall into the hands of the U.S. nor be taken over by it.

Avoiding the Worst Pitfalls

There are so many potential pitfalls confronting this country that one hardly knows which ones to worry about the most. The breakup of the country and its absorption by the U.S. would undoubtedly rank as the greatest risk in the minds of many people. And yet, there are clearly some who would not be bothered by either of these possibilities. A significant minority in Québec already wants out. Many English Canadians in other parts of the country are so fed up with the separatist threat that they are ready to call their bluff. There are still other Canadians who wouldn't care much if we did become part of the U.S.

The thought of this country disintegrating and falling

into the hands of the U.S. is a primary concern to me. But I have other concerns that run almost as deep. Most of these can be boiled down to one overriding one. That relates to the need to preserve the hierarchy of values and institutions with which I began in this volume. World trends are anything but encouraging when it comes to the maintenance of the combination of a liberal democratic system and mixed free enterprise or modified capitalistic economic order in which I believe.

I think it's going to take a lot of dedicated effort to preserve our kind of society. We are going to have to work hard at some of our social priorities and include more of them in our fundamental Western values if we want to preserve the more traditional ones such as freedom of speech and assembly. On the economic front, we are going to have to strive to reform what is left of our enterprise and collective bargaining systems if we are not to lose them both. But the greatest challenge of all probably lies in the political sphere. If we cannot revitalize our political processes in a manner which attracts a better caliber of person to public life in this country, then nothing else will matter.

Conclusion

The most frustrating thing about this great country of ours is the difference between its actual and its potential performance. No other country in the world has as much going for it, and yet we are far from exploiting all our advantages. In every sense, socially, economically, and politically, we are well below our capacity.

It is not so much by design that our actual performance has fallen so short of our potential. It is more by default.

There is so much we could be doing to rectify this situation. It is procrastination which is hurting us. Yet the more we delay, the more difficult the necessary decisions seem to become.

I am convinced Canada can begin to realize its potential in relatively short order. I have written this volume as a result of this conviction. It is not meant as a blueprint or a panacea, but I think it does offer a lot of common sense. I can only hope and trust that it will contribute to the rejuvenation which is required to make this country what it is capable of becoming.

Index